Praise For
Brick by Brick

Brick by Brick is a book that is written at a critical moment in church history in the United States. Trevor courageously discusses real challenges in the Church with great care, humility, and depth. In an era of extremes, confusion, and hopelessness, Brick by Brick offers a path forward, a path to be built! This book is more than must-read; it is an essential read.

—Grant Twyman
Director of Equity, K-12 public school district
COO, Next Consulting Firm
Captain, United States Army Reserve

***

I have had the honor of knowing Trevor for over a decade. Through the years, he has been steadfast in his integrity and obedience to where God is leading him and his family. I believe this book is so important for our churches. Do I agree with every word? No. But I wholeheartedly agree that these conversations need to be happening within church leadership. As Americans, I believe we've lost touch with nuanced conversations, and hopefully, this book will bring to light topics to help guide you to the truth. If you have been hurt by the church, may this read be a refreshing perspective of the *heart* of the Church. That we learn to follow the way of Jesus, together.

—Keana Zoradi
Deacon of Women
Creative Director at Awaken Retreat

Forty years ago, I would not have believed I would one day say this: "Sometimes it feels like the American church at large is lost." Today, it's not just me. For many, it's reached a breaking point. I get it. I feel their frustration. I understand why so many are wavering. It's why I'm so enthusiastic about Brick by Brick. Trevor explains this struggle. In his opening chapter, he writes, "Giving up "church" altogether isn't an option it is a biblical mandate. However, the way we are currently doing "church" in the 21st century has been exposed to be faulty at best." We know that the Church will be fine, our Savior says as much, but that doesn't mean there isn't work to be done. Trevor emphasizes these points by addressing many of the difficult issues the Church faces today. We need to double down on abiding in the Father, Son, and Holy Spirit. Our only hope is and will always be God…not the methods, mayhems, or manias in which we've become so enchanted. Brick by Brick is a necessary work.

—Ricki Lee Brooks
Pastor, West Sound Community Church

As someone who spent years in vocational ministry and now works in the secular realm, this book has helped me process much of the disillusionment that I wrestle with from my experiences. I value the theologically driven solutions that are presented in these chapters. Trevor is driven by a deep love for the Bride of Christ, and his words echo this passion. His courage to discuss the current state of the Church is much needed. I pray we use the scriptural insight in this book to help us rebuild what is broken.

—Justin Henderson
Former Pastor

Trevor does something amazing in this book, that everyone needs to do; ask hard questions. Specifically, of the western church. While you may not come to all the same conclusions as Trevor, I hope you follow his example of asking the tough questions and using the Bible to guide your answers. Trevor does that masterfully in these pages which is why you need to read this book.

—Mark Knight
Author of "Non-Anxious Churches: Finding the Way of Jesus for Pastors and Churches Today"
Pastor, Praise Covenant Church

Brick by Brick

Reconstructing the Deconstructed

Trevor Whitman

Published by KHARIS PUBLISHING, imprint of KHARIS MEDIA LLC.

Copyright © 2022 Trevor Whitman

ISBN-13: 978-1-63746-163-1

ISBN-10: 1-63746-163-1

Library of Congress Control Number: 2022943068

All KHARIS PUBLISHING products are available at special quantity discounts for bulk purchases for sales promotions, premiums, fund-raising, and educational needs. For details, contact:

Kharis Media LLC
Tel: 1-479-599-8657
support@kharispublishing.com
www.kharispublishing.com

Table of Contents

Who am I?

A question that plagues human existence from the moment we achieve consciousness to the day we die. We mull over this question in almost every decision we make. From the simple, "what kind of food do I like to eat?" to the more complex, "What do I stand for or against?"

Most of the time, people don't even know why they believe what they believe. To dig through the many layers that create our being, we must evaluate every part of us, including our motivations. Our fears and our desires take an enormous amount of time and self-reflection to understand. A simple term that describes a representation of all these things, is called our "worldview."

When it comes to generalizations about our worldview, they can be easy to identify. Where we lean politically, how we view the family unit, and what we think about foreign policy. These are normal talking points, to which if someone asked what our views were on such topics, we'd be able to rattle off a response. But our worldviews are so much deeper. They are the intricate and deeply complex source of literally everything we do and why we do them.

Where we get our worldviews is even more complex than the views themselves.

When describing to someone how our worldviews are formed both intentionally and subconsciously, I like to use the image of a brick house.

At the time of birth, our existence is an empty plot of land. Our worldviews are not determined by DNA. They are learned through experiences, what we are taught, what we observe, and who we observe throughout our life. This empty plot of land has the potential to be built in any different shape or form, but that ground tilling is initially done by those who raise us.

As young people, especially in our toddler years, our foundations are formed around family dynamics. Most of this is learned through observation and repetition. When looking at human growth and development, this is the period of time that can be described as the most formational and the foundation of who we become as people.

To this point, all our development has been in the hands of other people, primarily those who raise us. The ground was tilled in rudimentary years and our foundation was shaped and formed mainly through observation of the people in our immediate families. This is where the building begins, and humans begin taking more ownership over the development of their worldview. At this point, bricks begin to be laid both intentionally and unintentionally as we grow up.

Each brick that is laid, either consciously or unconsciously, develops how we view the world. Our upbringing, our experiences (good or bad), what we are explicitly taught, what we learn, where we learn from, who we learn from, observing behavior, testing boundaries, all these components are bricks that are placed to develop our worldview during our childhood and adolescence. When people reach adulthood, it becomes very difficult to change their minds about long-held beliefs consistent with their worldview.

As adults, the only way that our brick house changes is by intentionally choosing to be open to new information, having an open mind, and developing new thought patterns. This is possible, but it can never be done all at once. This process has become more popular in recent years and in most circles, it is referenced as "deconstruction." To continue the illustration, this is the process of observing a brick, noticing its faults, and removing the brick from the house. Within this process, there can be many healthy components that can lead to a deeper understanding and recognition of many faults in the entire house. But how we engage with this process needs to be done with great care and attention.

If our focus is only on deconstruction, we eventually will end up with a house that eventually falls. You can only take out so many bricks before the integrity of the whole building collapses. It is imperative that if we are taking bricks out, we are finding new and more sturdy bricks to replace them with. Staying in the downward spiral of deconstruction is easy. Sitting in the uncomfortable, removing bricks, and then replacing them with better ones is substantially more difficult and requires a greater level of patience not only with yourself but other people that are in the process as well.

You may be asking yourself, "What does this have to do with the Church and the main focus of this book?" Part of our brick house, if we are followers of Christ, is how we view and engage as the Body of Christ in the Church. Through our upbringing, experiences, and what we were taught, we have developed a worldview and ideology of "how the Church is supposed to work and operate." And because most of those bricks that were laid because "that's just how we've always done it," those bricks have largely gone unchallenged.

In recent years, this has not been the case. The reason why "deconstruction" has been a popular catchphrase the last few years in evangelical circles is that people have begun questioning the bricks that have been laid in their houses. Seeing news story after story of rampant abuse, church splits and divisions ravaging congregations, political ideologies taking over the pulpit, and inconsistent application of biblical principles among spiritual leaders, people have begun questioning if what the church is doing is even worth the trouble.

We are commanded in Scripture to never give up meeting together and we are described as the "Bride of Christ." Giving up "church" altogether isn't an option, it is a biblical mandate. However, the way we are currently doing "church" in the 21st century has been exposed to be faulty at best. So where do we go from here? This book is not meant to sway you towards any single secondary doctrine, nor does it have all the answers for "how we should do everything." The main effort being outlined through these chapters is for us to identify broken bricks, evaluate them honestly, remove them if necessary and replace them with bricks that align closer to God's intention for our meetings together.

Before engaging with the specific topics that will be covered, groundwork must be laid. Nothing in this book will put into question or cast doubt on Christ being our cornerstone (Ephesians 2:20) or the core of orthodoxy as our foundation. To consider oneself a Christian and a follower of Christ, we must uphold those two truths. Simply put, we believe that Christ is who He says He is: The Son of God and Savior for mankind. The core of orthodoxy is summed up well within the Apostle's Creed:

I believe in God, the Father almighty, creator of heaven and earth.

I believe in Jesus Christ, his only Son, our Lord, who was conceived by the Holy Spirit and born of the Virgin Mary.

He suffered under Pontius Pilate, was crucified, died, and was buried; he descended to hell.

On the third day, he rose again from the dead.

He ascended to heaven and is seated at the right hand of God the Father almighty.

From there He will come to judge the living and the dead.

I believe in the Holy Spirit, the Holy Church, the communion of saints, the forgiveness of sins, the resurrection of the body, and the life everlasting. Amen.

With those immovable truths set in stone, we are left with the remaining bricks within our house that lead to our worldview and ideologies for how the church is run and how it should operate. These bricks have come from our parents, our teachers, pastors, experiences, trauma, and education (or lack thereof).

Anyone that has been in or been a part of leading a church for any length of time acknowledges that there are broken aspects of how it operates. A part of this that needs to be addressed is that because the Church is being run by broken and sinful people, it comes as no surprise that aspects of the Church are going to be broken and sinful. This book is not intended to throw it all out. There are many beautiful aspects of the Church that should be replicated and celebrated, but there are equally as many aspects that are abusive, dark, and broken that need to be observed, removed, and replaced with bricks that are closer to what God intended.

When engaging in these types of conversations it is important to define the terms that will be used. There are two ways that "church" can be defined; one is lower-case "C" church which is a descriptor of one local specific congregation. Upper-case "C" Church refers to the universal Church which encapsulates all believers. This book is going to be addressing a hybrid of the two which is specifically the American Church. Not all issues that are brought up in this book apply to other churches around the world but could still lead to productive conversations about the state of churches elsewhere.

Lastly, it is encouraging to note that this book is not the "end all be all" or even the first to address such issues. There are even examples in Scripture where leaders felt the need to deconstruct their current paradigm to build up a new one that represented the Lord's heart for His people.

Elijah, in 1 Kings 18 removed bricks and replaced them with new ones, in a manner that was both physical and metaphorical in the destruction of the altar of Baal. Ahab who was the King of Israel at the time and the Kings before him abandoned the Lord's commands and worshiped the Baals. At the time of chapter 18, King Ahab was pursuing Elijah in an attempt to kill him because he was a known prophet of the Lord. When Elijah confronted Ahab, he challenged him to show which god was real, the Baals, or the one true God. After the people had gathered, Baals' prophets set up an altar for their sacrifice and Elijah reassembled the broken altar that had been there previously. In verses 30-31 Elijah is said to have repaired the altar that was once pleasing to the Lord but was currently in ruins. He replaced the ruins with twelve stones that represented the tribes of Israel and when it was finished placed his sacrifice on it.

For those familiar with that account, the prophets of Baal cry out to their false god to have him show himself powerful but had no success. Elijah then prays to the Lord and the Lord engulfs the sacrifice in fire to show Himself once again to His people and they cry out "The Lord-He is God!" (v.39)

This illustration perfectly illustrates the heart behind this book. Much like Elijah, he found himself looking at the ruins of an altar that was once pleasing to the Lord but had over time come to ruin. Maybe from neglect, maybe from time, or even intentional destruction, the altar was not what it once was. In the same way, the way America has constructed the modern-day church is not the same one that we read about in the New Testament.

Many have given in to the thought that, "Because it has always been this way, there is no other way to do it." They see the flaws, the ruin, the destruction, but because that is how they've experienced church their whole lives, they think that this must be the only way. This book is not intended to give a "one size fits all, here's how you do everything the right way according to Trevor." It simply is allowing you to examine specific issues that are currently plaguing the church, analyze what Scripture says about it, ponder the implications and applications, and deciding whether that "brick" in your worldview needs to be replaced or if it is okay where it is at.

Just like Elijah felt the need to rebuild from what once was into what it was meant to be. I believe the Church in America in the 21st century can deconstruct the aspects of the church that are leading to abuse, marginalization, idolization, and sin, by replacing them with systemic pieces that look more like what Christ intended for His body.

I hope that in you reading this book, you would be encouraged that others see the same issues that you might, but also give you the tools necessary to help bring solutions to your local church. It is always easy to point out problems, but it is substantially more difficult to be a part of the solution. My prayer is that as you breach each topic, you'd pray and ask the Lord to open your ears to hear and your eyes to see His heart for each item brought up, asking Him for wisdom and discernment to help you evaluate each issue individually.

Our process of evaluating bricks, determining whether they are good, and replacing them if need be is a continual process and never stops. Because we live in a broken and sinful world, our tendency is always going to be to fall back into old patterns and stray from God's intentions. This book is meant to be a starting point to edifying conversations and put the Church on a path of healthy gathering as God's people. As I dive into these topics, know that I too am constantly in process and am right alongside you with my desire to follow the Lord and His will for my life, let's pursue healthy gathering together.

Chapter 1

Celebrity Pastors and Our Desire for a King

Brick:

How does our current society "celebratize" pastors? Where does our desire to elevate our pastoral leaders on a pedestal come from? How is our desire for a "King" idolatrous? What does celebrity culture in the Church lead to? What is the role of a pastor and what should their attention be focused on?

Reason for analysis:

The current climate of pastoring in the United States has shifted significantly in the 21st century. A role that once focused around serving a community, shepherding a flock, and leading by example has led to a vocation that leads to power, influence, and celebrity. Not all pastors follow this path, but because this has come to be what is expected, pastors are pressured to write books, speak at conferences, and build a brand rather than shepherd what God has entrusted to them. There are plenty of pastors who are faithful to pastor their congregation, but it is becoming more and more common for some to strive after and achieve a level of celebrity that the world would recognize and celebrate. How we view the role of "pastor" has shifted in a way that needs to be observed and analyzed if what we are seeing now is what God desires from the leaders in that role.

1 Samuel 8-15

God's original design for a Kingdom can be seen in early Israel. In the beginning, 12 tribes were all descendants of Jacob who were led by Joshua during the conquest of Canaan. Once Joshua died, the dynamic of leadership in Israel shifted. Each of the tribes had its own leadership structure, but God would appoint Judges to lead Israel when they had been disobedient and surrounding nations would attack them, resulting in them crying out for God to save them. At that point, God appointed Judges over all of the nation, while still having resident leaders in charge of local issues. Within this structure, there was delegated leadership, but God was still the "King."

Time after time, Israel would return to their evil ways and in each instance, the Lord saved them by appointing a judge. The ultimate authority for the fate of Israel rested in God's hands. After a period, the Israelites grew weary of how things were being run. In 1 Samuel 8, Samuel appointed his sons to be judges over Israel and they began to pervert the position by accepting bribes and pursuing dishonest gain. At which point the elders came with a request for a King like the surrounding nations had. God's response to Samuel's prayers was sobering:

"And the Lord told him: "Listen to all that the people are saying to you; it is not you they have rejected, but they have rejected me as their king. As they have done from the day I brought them up out of Egypt until this day, forsaking me and serving other gods, so they are doing to you. Now listen to them; but warn them solemnly and let them know what the king who will reign over them will do." (1 Samuel 8:7-9)

The request from the elders was extremely shortsighted. They wanted someone who was a physical representation of the leadership they desired, instead of trusting an invisible God whom only a select few were allowed to interact with. Samuel attempted to show them that if they got what they were asking for, they essentially would become slaves to their new king. The elders cast that warning aside and demanded a King anyway.

At this point, the Lord finally relented to the complaints that had plagued Israel for generations and gave them what they asked for. The Lord wanted to remain their King, but true to His character, He wasn't going to force Himself upon them. And so, Samuel anointed Saul as the first King of Israel. As you read further into the historical accounts of Kings throughout Israel's lineage and as both God and Samuel tried to warn them, the results were terrible. Samuel in chapter 12 describes the Israelites' request for a king as "evil" and rebukes Saul in chapter 13 because Saul relied on his wisdom and knowledge to lead Israel instead of obeying the Lord's commands, which led to disaster. There was a long line of both righteous and wicked Kings and Israel was constantly in a state of flux depending on who was in leadership at the time. Samuel puts it aptly in chapter 13 when he says, "But when you saw that Nahash king of the Ammonites was moving against you, you said to me, '"No, we want a king to rule over us' even though the Lord your God was your king." (v.12) The Israelites already had everything they needed with the Lord as their King but thought they should look like the world around them, and it led exactly where Samuel and the Lord warned them it would.

As much as we'd hope that the same desire for a king would begin and end in the Old Testament, we, unfortunately, see it spring up in the New Testament as well, just in a different way. Early followers of Christ after Jesus' death debated which of the teachers they'd follow (Paul or Apollos - 1 Cor. 1) and they had to be corrected. In Paul's writings to the church in Ephesus and the church in Colossae, Paul depicts the same breakdown in logic that Samuel had to deal with, and Paul addresses it bluntly.

Paul breaks it down three ways:

- In Ephesians 5:23, "For the husband is the head of the wife as Christ is the head of the church, his body, of which he is the Savior."
- Colossians 1:18, "And He is the head of the body, the church; He is the beginning and the firstborn from among the dead so that in everything He might have the supremacy."
- Ephesians 1:22-23, "And God placed all things under his feet and appointed him to be head over everything for the church, which is his body, the fullness of him who fills everything in every way."

To put it frankly, Paul tells the churches in Ephesus and Colossae that it is not Paul or Apollos that leads the Church, it is Christ. The believers in the New Testament struggled with the same thing the Israelites did in the Old Testament. They desired a physical representation of leadership that they could look to and elevate when instead they should realize that having God as their ultimate authority is by design the best thing for them.

The inner struggle that the Church finds itself in now is nothing new. However, the biggest difference is that we have examples of the Old and New Testaments to help us not follow the same path. Man's desire for a "king" other than Christ still manifests today in our celebrity pastor culture.

These leaders get placed on a pedestal that is virtually impossible for them to upkeep. The only individual that is capable of holding such a mantle is Christ. That is the beginning and the end of the list of anyone worthy of a pedestal. Though we have different giftings/anointings, that does not elevate any of us above each other. In the body, we all have a role to play and some of those roles are more public-facing than others, but that does not make any one person greater than another. The problem with being placed on a pedestal is that the higher that pedestal goes, the further one can fall.

How do believers in today's day and age contribute to this issue of pastors reaching celebrity status? Just like it wasn't "bad" or "wrong" for believers in the NT to follow Apollos' or Paul's teachings, it isn't "bad" or "wrong" for believers to follow teachers now. Where things begin to get out of whack is when those teachers are elevated above the teachings of Christ and are either teaching new/skewed doctrine, or their teachings become more prevalent than the teachings of Christ themselves.

How much control does a pastor have in how congregants/believers view them? Especially in the last ten to twenty years, the "pastoral track" seems to follow a similar trajectory. Get into ministry, rise to the position of "head pastor," gain larger numbers of congregants, begin writing books, go on speaking tours, start a podcast, eventually move out of the head pastor role, gain a wide-scale audience, and influence large swaths of people. None of these elements are "wrong" or "sinful" in and of themselves, but this path produces this celebrity culture, where believers are wrapped up in what pastors are saying, what books they are releasing, what new content they are producing, and focused solely on that leader's works. This looks eerily similar to how celebrity culture works in the world.

When this type of situation takes place, it can be easy to replace the teachings of Christ with what this individual says. Instead of these teachings being a supplement to our relationship with Christ, it takes its place of it. Similarly, the request for a King by the Israelites or a lead teacher by the early church, our natural sinful inclination is to seek a leader that we can tangibly see and follow rather than seek and follow Christ. When we do this, intentionally or not, that individual becomes an idol in our lives that we supplant as our faux-Christ rather than God Himself. Instead of leading people to Christ, they lead people to themselves. Pastors of a church should not be pursuing celebrity; they should be pastoring their congregation.

What is the role of a "pastor"? First, it is important to distinguish the difference between those who have the spiritual gift of teaching and the spiritual gift of pastoring. All too often those spiritual gifts are combined when churches are looking for new pastors to hire, when, having both and doing both with excellence is rare. In Ephesians 4:11-13, Paul lists out some of the spiritual giftings or roles that need to be filled in the Church, "It was he who gave some to be apostles, some to be prophets, some to be evangelists, and some to be pastors and teachers, to prepare God's people for works of service, so that the body of Christ may be built up until we all reach unity in the faith and the knowledge of the Son of God and become mature, attaining to the whole measure of the fullness of Christ."

The gift of teaching is exactly that, the ability to teach. But not just standing on a stage with a microphone. There is more of an art to teaching that people with this specific spiritual gifting have. They have a way of sharing stories in a way that everyone can relate to. Breaking down complex concepts in ways that anyone from any background can understand. Providing real-life illustrations that stick with people in their everyday lives. Everyone has had a teacher like that, whether in school, in a church, or even in a YouTube video. People that possess the gift of teaching help people learn in deep and lasting ways. But just because someone is a gifted teacher, does not inherently mean that they would be a good pastor.

The inverse is true as well. Just because someone is a good pastor does not mean that they are inherently a good teacher. A synonym for "pastor" is "shepherd of a flock" which holds strong imagery throughout Scripture and the word "pastor" translated from Paul's writings comes from a word that means, "to shepherd." In 1 Peter 5:2-3, Peter describes the role of shepherds, by saying, "Be shepherds of God's flock that is under your care, serving as overseers-not because you must, but because you are willing, as God wants you to be; not greedy for money, but eager to serve; not lording it over those entrusted to you, but being examples to the flock."

Being a pastor or shepherd of a church is a calling. The way that Peter explains it in his writing is spot on. It must be something you do because you are willing to serve, not because you must, and not because of the money that is involved. He also goes as far as to point out the power dynamic that comes with the territory of being a spiritual leader among people, instructing them not to "lord it over" the people that they are serving. Taking on the mantle of being a pastor is no simple task, nor should it be accepted lightly. This position and expression of the spiritual gift of pastoring are designed for individuals that deeply care for the needs of their church. These caretakers walk with the body they've been tasked to oversee through everything. Trauma, joy, victories, defeat, lean times, and plentiful times, through strength and weakness, pastors walk through it all. This type of work is not glamorous, it isn't attractive, and it isn't for the faint of heart, which is why this must be a calling.

Anyone that uses the platform and title of "pastor" to advance themselves, build a brand, expand influence, gain power, and curate a following is perverting the true intention of the role. The pursuit of power in a spiritual position was fully fleshed out by the Pharisees and Sadducees operating in the nation of Israel before Christ came. Up until Jesus' arrival, Israel operated under the leadership of prophets and priests. Priests were the only ones who were able to be in the presence of God and interact with Him. When the veil was torn upon Jesus' death and the Holy Spirit was sent among believers at Pentecost, the entire power dynamic of the Kingdom on earth changed drastically.

In 1 Peter 2:9, believers are described as God's "chosen people, a royal priesthood, a holy nation, a people belonging to God, that you may declare the praises of him who call you out of darkness into his wonderful light." In the Old Testament, the Israelites had to depend on priests to advocate on their behalf before God, because none of them were holy enough before God to interact with Him themselves. Humanity is still not holy enough to engage with the King of all Kings, but because of the sacrifice of Jesus and the blessing of the

Holy Spirit, we no longer need an intermediary from humanity, because Jesus is our permanent liaison between us and the Father.

With this new dynamic in place, all of humanity was placed on a level playing field again. No longer were there some people with higher stature in the eyes of God than others. If someone claims Christ as their Lord and Savior and follows Him, they are considered a part of the "royal priesthood" and there is no higher position than that. No matter what role or position someone has in the Kingdom here on Earth, God views all believers through the same lens, holy and righteous priests who are justified through Christ's sacrifice.

This paradigm is what creates issues with the "celebrity" culture that has developed in the United States in particular. Pastoral ministry is not meant for the limelight. The position demands the service of the body and the caretaking of its congregation. This is virtually impossible with the current standards set by those who have achieved celebrity status with book deals, seminars, conferences, interviews, etc.

There is nothing wrong with writing books or keynoting seminars, however by holding a position that is specifically designed to care for a congregation, one has a responsibility to them to shepherd and guide those people. This is where it might be beneficial to have more people fill one role rather than one person holding many. Within any given congregation, there may be 3 to 4 qualified teachers and speakers that would adequately bring the Word on Sunday and 3 to 4 separate people who are called more to pastoral ministry. Distilling down positions based on who is paid or who has higher status is what prevents more people from using the strengths and gifts that the Lord has bestowed on them.

As believers and followers of Christ, seeking celebrity, followers, or fame is not Gospel-centric. Jesus was radically counter-cultural in this way, where He advised those who followed Him to put others above themselves, humble themselves and serve others. Paul is even more explicit by saying in Philippians 2:3, "Do not act out of selfish ambition or conceit, but with humility think of others as being greater than yourselves."

Because of the age we find ourselves in, it has never been easier to build an audience, create a following of thousands, if not millions, and become a celebrity almost overnight. Social media, podcasts, and electronic books make it so that someone can reach out and influence huge amounts of people all at the same time. This is both a blessing and a curse. Someone could use that kind of reach for the gospel and help people on a wide scale, but one post later push their agenda, leverage their influence for ad revenue and build their brand. Discipling of people was never meant to be done on a scale of millions of people and balancing this line is something that only this generation of believers has had to deal with. There is no instruction manual and no history to look back on. The reach pastors have online has never been greater than it is today. If Jesus while here on Earth only took on discipling 12 people directly, the thought of discipling thousands or even millions of people at the same time is preposterous.

This is where it is helpful to bring distinction between those who seek to teach and those who seek to pastor and do their best to not overlap if teaching to millions in the world is their end goal. If someone builds a following as a teacher, utilizing social media, and building a following simply for the sake of teaching and preaching, that is one thing. But if someone is a pastor of a church and attempts to seek the same kind of following, that pastor is missing the point of why they are a pastor, to begin with. Pastors are meant to be shepherds of a flock and disciplers of congregants, not influencers and best-selling authors.

Although pastors are called to shepherd God's people from passages in the New Testament, that title is also present in the Old Testament. God oftentimes refers to those who lead Israel as shepherds of His people. That imagery is drawn upon many times, and specifically, in Jeremiah 23, God speaks harshly to these leaders who have enabled their people to go astray. "Woe to the shepherds who are destroying and scattering the sheep of my pasture!" declares the Lord. Therefore, this is what the Lord, the God of Israel, says to the shepherds who tend my people: "Because you have scattered my flock and driven them away and have not bestowed care on them, I will bestow punishment on you for the evil you have done," declares the Lord. I will gather the remnant of my flock out of all the countries where I have driven them and will bring them back to their pasture, where they will be fruitful and increase in number. I will place shepherds over them who will tend them, and they will no longer be afraid or terrified, nor will any be missing," declares the Lord." (v.1-4)

God takes the role of a shepherd very seriously. Whether that be with His people in the Old Testament, the Israelites, or His people after the death and resurrection of Christ, His body, how those who have been called to shepherd go about leading His flock is to be taken seriously. One of the ways that shepherds allowed the Israelites to stray is eerily similar to shepherds who allowed their flocks to stray in late 2020.

Later in Jeremiah 23, in verses 25-40, God declares his utter disgust with false prophets and oracles. Describing how prophets and oracles have spoken in His name, but with no revelation from Him. The reason why this is such a big deal is that speaking false prophecy is blasphemy, which is one of the most egregious ways of offending God. When someone speaks on His behalf, that is to be done in reverence, humility, and boldness, and can never be wrong. Verses 25-32 sum up how God feels about false prophets who have infiltrated His people and allowed by leaders who were charged with shepherding His people:

"I have heard what the prophets say who prophesy lies in my name. They say, 'I had a dream! I had a dream!'" How long will this continue in the hearts of these lying prophets, who prophesy the delusions of their minds? They think the dreams they tell one another will make my people forget my name, just as their fathers forgot my name through Baal worship. Let the prophet who has a dream tell his dream, but the one who has my word speak it faithfully. For what has straw to do with grain?" declares the Lord, "Is not my word like fire," declares the Lord, "and like a hammer that breaks a rock in pieces? Therefore," declares the Lord, "I am against the prophets who steal from one another words supposedly from me. Yes," declares the Lord, "I am against the prophets who wag their own tongues and yet declare, 'The Lord declares.' Indeed, I am against those who prophesy false dreams,' declares the Lord. "They tell them and lead my people astray with their reckless lies, yet I did not send or appoint them. They do not benefit these people in the least," declares the Lord."

The same issue that plagued the Israelites during this time and others throughout the Old Testament is what is deceiving His people now. Pastors, but especially celebrity pastors with large amounts of influence found themselves in a time when a lot of people were looking to them for guidance. The election season of 2020 was one of the most contentious and divisive elections in recent history. When people were hungry to be led and shepherded, the danger of the celebratization of pastors came to fruition.

There were countless instances of false prophecy that occurred in a short few months. Pastors with influence over millions of people were declaring from their pulpits all kinds of prophecies, dreams, and "words from God" that never came to fruition. This cannot be overlooked! When someone claims that they are speaking on behalf of God about the direction of a nation or events that are to come or words of correction, they must be right one hundred percent of the time. If they are wrong, that means they are either speaking from their flesh or from the influence of a spirit that is not the Holy Spirit. This would already be a massive issue if it was on a smaller scale and to a less attended congregation. But when celebrity pastors have the platform that they do, and the followers that they have, these false prophecies can and did spread like wildfire. The result was both embarrassing for believers and identified a gigantic problem within this new context of celebrity pastors and their huge followings that history has never seen.

When one person has a platform that large and is charged with tending that entire flock as their shepherd, it simply cannot be done. It isn't how the Church was initially built in the New Testament and it isn't how the Church is supposed to operate now. There were times that there were large gatherings and thousands of people would come to Christ, but those were one-off events and led by traveling missionaries and teachers. The work that we see from people like Timothy in Scripture was to take these recent converts and lead them in a smaller context as a pastor and within a congregation.

Both congregants and pastors have built the paradigm that exists today. On one side, congregants expect their pastors to act like celebrity pastors they see on their favorite social media platforms and pursue similar paths. And on the other, pastors put that same pressure on themselves to do more than what they were called to do. This, among other things, leads to pastors being placed on a pedestal, where it becomes more important to have large amounts of followers, flashy lights, and bite-sized teachings than to leading people to real freedom, discipling them through all seasons and focusing on the overall health of their flock.

This desire to have a celebrity pastor at the center of a movement spawns from the same place the Israelites and the Early Church came from. Our inherent sinful nature desires a physical representation of leadership that we can follow, rather than following the One True King. God desires for us to follow Him and Him alone. This is both in leadership and in guidance, where we don't look to any one person to lead us solely, but instead, follow Christ first and anything else is supplemental. Pastors are equipped to shepherd people, by facilitating opportunities for people to interact with God Himself and empower them to live out the calling in their lives. When this is on too large of a scale, it becomes impossible for that pastor to appropriately shepherd the people entrusted to them. Our desire should align with God's desire, which is to look to Him as our one and only King, follow what He has called us to do, and not elevate any one person higher than they ought to be.

Chapter 2

Prosperity Gospel

Brick:

What does our relationship with money say about our view of God? What role should wealth and prosperity play in our mindset as believers? How can the desire for money change the way we live our lives as believers or meet together as congregations? How can our view of righteousness change if we elevate wealth to an inappropriately high pedestal in our lives? What should we expect our lives to look like as followers of Christ according to the Word?

Reason for analysis:

The heresy of the prosperity gospel is not a new phenomenon. But with the rise of many mega-churches throughout the United States that prescribe this false theology, it has seeped into many churches that adopt a lot of the same principles. This type of doctrine being taught has led to a warped view of righteousness, where people are convinced that they will have earthly riches if they obey God and if they don't have physical wealth, they are not in good standing with God. Therefore, leading people to pursue wealth at any cost and at the expense of whoever it takes to get there. Teaching righteousness through this flawed lens also distorts how people treat the poor. If having wealth is the sign of righteousness and God's favor, then the inverse must also be true that being poor is a sign of wickedness and God's judgment. The way the Bible is taught within these congregations and how tithes are collected with words of guilt rather than being a joyful and inspired thing creates a false sense of superiority when someone does have wealth. Having money and material items is not a sign of "being on the right path," nor does it indicate God's favor. And yet, churches that subscribe to this theology continue to show partiality towards the rich, judgment of the poor, and teach that if you follow Christ that only wealth and prosperity will ensue. These principles are nowhere to be found in Scripture, and in most cases, it says the opposite. When people experience the dark side of this theology, the damage can be catastrophic. It leads people to question everything about themselves, including their faith, when they go through a hard time, that they believe if you are righteous, you should never have to endure. The prosperity gospel is dangerous, and believers should be wary of the many teachings that can very easily slip into a Sunday morning service.

The Bible has a lot to say about the role of wealth and riches. Both in how people throughout history have approached it and used or abused wealth and in teaching directly about it. We have examples like Solomon who experienced the very ends of wealth and describes his findings in the book of Ecclesiastes where the consensus is that nothing material will ever fulfill us. Jesus answers many questions about the role of wealth and consistently answers that it is easier to find and know Him when you are poor than when you are rich. And many warnings about what the love of money and the focus on wealth can lead to. This is why it is confusing to see so many preachers and pastors lean into the prosperity gospel when so much of Scripture says the exact opposite.

Righteousness being evaluated from worldly success leads to the "ends justify the means" ideology which is one of the sources of abusive cultures. If the generation of wealth is built upon the foundation of God's favor and righteousness, where the more you get, the more it is an indication you are on the right path, doing whatever it takes to accumulate more is the logical conclusion. And these types of pursuits always come at a cost, most of which are people. In this scenario people are used for what they have to offer, that resource is taken to elevate the church or pastor in some scenario and when their use is tapped out, they are cast aside to use someone else. The ends do not justify the means and having a warped view of righteousness makes it all the easier to treat people in this way. 1 Timothy 6:10 says that "The love of money is a root of all kinds of evil." To be clear, it is not saying that the love of money is the root of all evil, as is often misquoted, but just all kinds. This means, that if someone loves money and the pursuit of wealth, all kinds of evil can come from that pursuit. Money should be seen as a useful tool, but as Psalm 62:10 says, we should not set our hearts on it.

Paul also tells Timothy later in chapter 6, "None of our hope should come from riches, but in God who provides" (v.17). There is a reason why Jesus says it is harder for a rich man to enter heaven than for a camel to be threaded through the eye of a needle (Matt. 19:16-30). He isn't saying that rich people can't be saved. But if you have wealth, it is much easier to depend on your resources and ability to provide for yourself in times of need than when someone who is strapped financially must depend on the Lord to provide for their every need. When people are in trouble, when they are in need, when they are struggling, that is when the Lord very tangibly provides. It is much easier to point to the times that the Lord came through in your life if the only explanation is that the Lord did it, rather than using your wealth to solve those same problems. Again, it is not saying that wealthy people are incapable of seeing or experiencing God, just that it is much harder to trust and believe in Him when you can solve problems yourself.

In Matthew 6:24, Jesus points out that man cannot serve both God and money by saying that we can only have one master. What or who do we trust when times are hard? What or who do we turn to for comfort when we are in pain or struggling? Where do we go when the world is against us, and circumstances aren't going our way? You will either go to the Lord or some deviation of wealth, material items, or something you can buy. Revelation 3:17 says it well when John says, "For you say, I am rich, I have prospered, and I need nothing, not realizing that you are wretched, pitiable, poor, blind and naked." Worldly wealth can provide a false sense of security as it pertains to our eternal lives. It may make us comfortable here on earth in many ways, but it can keep you blind to the fact that you are spiritually bankrupt and empty in ways that matter. A statement that rings true to this type of problem is that "If you can solve a problem with a check, that's not a problem." There are problems far greater that can't be solved with any sum of money. The problem is not having wealth, Jesus never says having wealth is wicked or wrong, it is the heart's space and views towards that wealth that can lead to sin.

To address this heart space, Paul continues in 1 Timothy 6:9 saying, "But those who desire to be rich fall into temptation, into a snare, into many senseless and harmful desires that plunge people into ruin in destruction." And one of the excerpts of Solomon's writings in Ecclesiastes 5:10 expresses that, "He who loves money will not be satisfied by money..." Over and over and over again the Bible writes that the love, desire, and soulless pursuit of great wealth will never fulfill you. We can trust that Solomon is a worthy source when he gains literally every ounce of worldly wealth for his time and still is left feeling unfulfilled. This is why when God offers Him anything in this world as a reward for his father's faithfulness, Solomon requests God's wisdom, knowing that there is no price tag on that. The pursuit of wealth is never-ending, there is no true satisfaction, and it will never be good enough. You ask the richest people in the world, whose focus is to constantly build for more of what they want, and they will always respond with "more."

Not only will money and wealth never fulfill you, but if your mentality revolves around wealth, it also tends to warp your view of other people as well. Even though verses like James 2:1-26 exist which strictly forbid Christians from showing partiality towards the rich over the poor, we still see it very blatantly carried out today. There was a podcast done in early 2021 by two women who used to work at one of the world's most well-known mega-churches who describe seating celebrities in places of honor and moving common people out of their seats to accommodate that like it was a concert or court side seats. Pushing a "less than" out of their seat, sometimes mid-service to seat someone rich and famous is literally the opposite of how believers are supposed to interact with people according to the Word.

Whether someone is rich or poor, God sees us and treats us all the same. In Proverbs 22:2, Solomon outlines that, "The rich and the poor meet together, the Lord is the maker of them all" and even says earlier in Proverbs 14:31, "Whoever oppresses a poor man insults his Maker, but he who is generous to the needy honors Him." Our relationships with people should never be dictated based on someone's wealth or status according to how the world outlines success. This type of mentality exists within the church in the United States, and it crosses many denominations. The elevation of wealth snuffs out the power of the truth. In Mark 4:19 at the end of the Parable of the Sower, Mark describes that the seed sown among the thorns (aka people who hear the word and reject it) turns away from the Lord largely because of the deceitfulness of wealth which chokes the word and makes it unfruitful.

Some churches blatantly teach that if you are rich that is a sign that God has blessed you because of your righteousness and if you are poor, that is a sign that God is judging and punishing you. Those types of messages and teachings are clearly the prosperity gospel and easy to identify. But it can rear its ugly head even in small ways like a small blurb of teaching before an offering is taken. Where the person speaking says something along the lines of "the more you give to the Church and to the Lord in the offering, the more blessing and favor He will pour out on you" which is substantially trickier to parse.

Understanding the nuance of those types of statements is what makes it difficult to see the prosperity gospel at play. Because on one hand, part of what they are saying is true. Which is that when you are obedient to the Lord and do what He has called you to do, He will make a path for you (Proverbs 3:5-6) and that He will care for your needs like He does for the birds of the air and the lilies of the field (Matthew 6:26-34). But that doesn't necessarily mean that the way the Lord makes for people is through wealth and earthly riches. Sometimes the Lord blesses people abundantly in ways that have nothing to do with the accumulation of money here on the earth. But the other part of the nuance within that type of statement before an offering is an assumption people make when hearing something like that, which is "the more they give to this specific church, in this specific offering, the more the Lord will give them in return." Some people give to the church, simply because they anticipate receiving more in return. They quickly find out, that the Lord is not an equation, where A+B does not = C, and can quickly find themselves in sticky situations financially because of how they gave at church. Now, to be clear, if the Lord asks us to give in a specific way, even if it is wild and outrageous, we are called to obey. But manipulating people before an offering, to get them to give more to the church, by promising they'll receive more financial riches in return, is spiritual manipulation and is wrong.

When we give our tithe, we are called to give with joyful hearts (2 Cor. 9) not out of guilt. This type of manipulation is nothing new. In the Middle Ages, the Catholic Church would sell indulgences that would supposedly absolve people of their sins or limit their time in purgatory. God does not need our money to do what He wants to do. Our tithe is more about our dependency and trust in Him than it is about the actual financial resources themselves. The prosperity gospel isn't just dangerous in theology and ideology, but also tangibly how we treat people.

If we view people in poverty as being there because of sin, that type of approach tends to lead to judgment instead of compassion. And the Bible is littered with verses discussing the need for followers of God to be compassionate and empathetic towards those in need. Jesus surrounded Himself with the marginalized, the poor, the desperate, and the needy and very clearly calls out those who believed themselves too good to be with Him. He says that He didn't come for the healthy but the sick (Mark 2:17). This is talking about those who believe themselves to be righteous when He came for those who are humble enough to admit their need for Him. This can be seen both spiritually and materially.

The prosperity gospel is dangerous first and foremost because the Bible teaches the exact opposite. Secondly, it pervades our congregations because it can lead to a severe crisis of faith when people go through hard situations and either believe that hard thing is happening because God is judging them, that they didn't give enough tithe, or that God doesn't love them, or any number of incorrect conclusions that come from holding a false theology like this. And lastly, it negatively impacts how we evangelize and treat those who are less fortunate and needy when we have a direct charge from God to treat them with dignity, respect, love, and help in ways that will lead them to Him. You cannot have an accurate view of people who are living in poverty if you believe in the prosperity gospel. So, what should our expectations be of our lives as believers, if it isn't to live in great wealth and prosperity according to worldly standards?

Instead of the never-ending pursuit of wealth, Scripture is clear that believers are called to a life of contentment. One of the most misquoted passages in all of the Bible is Philippians where Paul says in chapter 4, verse 13, "I can do all things through Christ who strengthens me." And although this sounds nice on a car bumper sticker and in theory, this feeds into the same hubris of the prosperity gospel. The reality is that God can do all things, but we cannot. There are limitations that we as humans have, and if taken too far, this type of theology can be both dangerous and harmful. There are things that we cannot do and that is all part of the human experience. If someone truly believes they can do anything, imagine the possible danger they could be in if they tested that to the extreme. The actual context of that verse is much more comforting, encouraging, and challenging to our everyday life as believers.

Verses 10-13 say, "I rejoiced greatly in the Lord that at last, you renewed your concern for me. Indeed, you were concerned, but you had no opportunity to show it. I am not saying this because I am in need, for I have learned to be content whatever the circumstances. I know what it is to be in need, and I know what it is to have plenty. I have learned the secret of being content in any and every situation, whether well fed or hungry, whether living in plenty or in want. I can do all this through him who gives me strength." The context of that last verse is that Paul is describing a state of being that is content in both seasons of plenty and want. Said in another way, Paul knows what it is like and is content with both being poor and being wealthy. This means that regardless of what situation or circumstance he may find himself in a worldly sense, Paul is content in all of them, because his relationship with God transcends any situation he could find himself in. We are called to live in a similar state of mind. Where we can worship God in seasons of plenty and want, trusting Him for our provision and knowing where all good things come from. A big reason why Paul most likely included this in his letter to Philippi is that he knew that believers that followed Christ would face all sorts of trials like he had in his mission to share the gospel.

Believers must accept the fact that we live in a broken world, and because we live in a world broken with sin, hardship and suffering will happen. This truth is not supposed to discourage us, but to give us clarity and proper expectations. If we believe that there will be no hardship or trials for us in this world and then there are, we will not be prepared. Believing in this way only sets you up for failure because

it is not a question of if you will experience hardship, it is when. The result of sin entering the world is that there will be suffering, pain, and death. Jesus promises us this in John 16:33, when He says, "In the world you will have tribulation. But take heart; I have overcome the world." In 2 Corinthians 6:3-10, Paul encourages believers to have endurance because believers will face afflictions, hardships, calamities, beatings, imprisonments, riots, labors, sleepless nights, and hunger and that through those situations we will gain purity, patience, knowledge, kindness, love, truthful speech, and the power of God with righteousness. God does not inflict these hardships, but He does use them to sanctify us, making us more like Him. Some hear these truths and allow themselves to go down a dark path only seeing the bad things, but the Lord redeems all of it for His glory.

Later in 2 Corinthians, in chapter 12 verses 9-10, Paul continues, encouraging the church of Corinth describing that "... I am content with weaknesses, insults, hardships, persecutions, and calamities. For when I am weak, then I am strong." He emphasizes again that a believer should not live in fear of hard times, but rather embrace them when they come to see the Lord work even more clearly in their lives. We can experience the fullness of the feeling of these moments, remembering that Jesus wept when his friend Lazarus died, even knowing that he would be resurrected. Jesus permits us to feel the weight of the pain of suffering and death but wants to be there ready to pick us back up when we are ready. Knowing that He can make all things work together for His glory. Life will come with seasons of sorrow and times of celebration and Paul encourages us to learn how to find contentment in all those seasons. He knows that happiness is fleeting and that our real goal should be to find joy.

As believers, we are called to find joy, regardless of circumstances. Happiness is a temporary feeling that leaves as fast as it comes. It is completely circumstantially dependent and depending on how certain things play out, you can be happy or sad, and sometimes those feelings don't even make sense. Striving for happiness leads to a roller coaster of emotions that is oftentimes hard to control. That is why we are called to find joy. Because joy is a choice, it is a state of mind and a place of being where regardless of the situation, we can find a reason to praise Him, always.

James describes joy in the context of trial when he says in chapter 1 verses 2-3 that we are called to consider it a joy to face trials of many kinds. Later describing those trials as a refining fire to make us into the people God created us to be. Paul talks about that joy coming from an unwavering trust in the Lord in Romans 15:13 when he says that not only joy but also peace come from hope that comes from the power of the Holy Spirit. And Peter talks about belief leading to being filled with inexpressible and glorious joy in 1 Peter 1:8-9. The choice to have belief, trust, and hope in the Lord, is what leads to a joy that transcends circumstance.

Believers don't need the promise of riches, wealth, and prosperity to live a joyous, fulfilled life. The prosperity gospel is a mirage of things that we are convinced by the world that we need and very obviously don't. Being allured by consumerism and the drive to always have the next best thing will never lead to true satisfaction and the ability to attain wealth and those material items say absolutely nothing about our righteousness. The Lord provides for our needs, He cares for our provision, but He says nothing of making all believers rich in a worldly sense if they follow Him. In fact, just like the rich young ruler in Matthew 19, the Lord often will ask us to abandon those worldly possessions and pursuits to follow Him. The prosperity gospel is an unfruitful heresy that needs to be weeded out from our theology and doctrine, so we can have a more accurate view of the world that only God can give us and find true joy in a relationship with Him.

Chapter 3

Consumerism

Brick:

How has the Church adopted the same consumerist tendencies that the world has? Why is consumerism not appropriate in the Church? How can consumerism dictate the direction and heart of a church? Why is it difficult for churches to keep consumerism out of their sermons, worship songs, and service structure?

Reason for analysis:

Over time many churches in the USA have become "Sunday-centric." Where the service on Sunday is the "end all, be all" that most of the resources churches have been dedicated to. This is because as a society, we have demanded that the church entertain us. This isn't overt, nor is it talked about often, but people tend to leave churches because of the experience on a Sunday morning and their preferences not being met. Having this expectation placed on them, church leadership is often pressured to add more to the experience on Sunday mornings to appease our culture's desire to be constantly entertained. This is achieved through a myriad of methods like smoke machines, lasers, concert-like worship, and shallow messages that can be seen as nothing more than a humanist motivational speech. Does every church look like this? No. But if given more resources, even the smallest of churches would strive to make their services more attractive. The difficulty with this reality is that these changes are normally made with good hearts. Those on staff want to do whatever they can to attract people into attending their church so they can hear The Good News. This is often referred to as the "seeker-sensitive" model. When churches operate this way, they encourage the consumerist tendencies that we see so prevalently in our country's culture, where people are more concerned about what they are getting out of attending a Sunday service than they are with how they are engaging as the body of Christ.

Throughout history, the Church has existed in a vast array of cultural moments. Depending on the country and place in history, a Christian's experience in their church and community looks very different from others. Each instance yields different challenges to overcome, and today's era is no different. As this book outlines, there are plenty of aspects to analyze, but one seems to be a common denominator throughout most churches in the United States in the 21st century.

Consumerism is the backbone of a capitalistic society like the United States. Supply and demand, the marketplace of ideas, and the "American Dream," all contribute to how citizens approach living in this country. It is impossible to avoid aspects of culture from seeping into the pews of the local church. Though we may try, holding firmly to verses where we are called to "live in the world, but not of the world," this ideal breaks down quickly because this mentality is woven into the fabric of how our society operates. As a people, in almost every area of our lives, we have been conditioned to expect everything we engage in to accommodate our every whim, desire, and preference. When events don't meet those expectations, we move on to something we think will. Living this way in our culture is deeply ingrained into our personas, to the point where we don't even notice. But functioning this way as a church has deep ramifications that ripple throughout every way local churches operate.

There have been many ways this phenomenon has been described in this modern era. Phrases like "church shopping" and "church hopping" are used when identifying people seeking a body that fits the preferences they have outlined as necessary for their attendance. These can range from the type of music that is played to the types of chairs they have in the auditorium, or if they even have an auditorium, to begin with! Living in a consumerist culture, we are constantly making decisions based on our preferences, and how people choose their church is no different. The problem with this consumerist mentality is that though it may be appropriate for how we operate in society, it exasperates our idolization of comfort as Christians. Our culture is obsessed with making everything as comfortable, easy, pain-free, and streamlined as possible. This type of emphasis cannot coexist with a gospel that guarantees difficulty and persecution along with the joy, peace, and fulfillment it provides. When things become uncomfortable, difficult, or not to our preference, we've been conditioned to leave.

With the constant influx of congregants coming and going, churches feel the pressure to appeal to the masses. This is done in a variety of ways, but this bending of oneself continues the cyclical nature of side growth. Not a lot of church growth comes from new salvations these days, it comes from people who used to attend one church, leaving to attend another. Someone deciding to leave a church because of preference will never be satisfied. There will always be some aspect to a service that people won't like, which is why trying to appease that insatiable hunger is fruitless. If the focus for the average attendee is "What do "I" get out of it?" the local church will continue to struggle with a "keeping up with the Joneses" type mentality of running services. Because this has largely been the focus of local churches, it has gradually changed how churches and their services are structured.

Church services have become an experience where you show up, enjoy music, sit, listen to a message, talk to a few people, and go home. But is this what has defined "church" throughout history? Is the local church meant to lean on only a few doing the spiritual heavy lifting and the rest of the congregation be spectators? The lack of commitment and investment from the body has led us to expect our leaders to live holy lives, for them to put on service for us to "get something out of" and then go about living our lives the rest of the week. But the church was never intended to be a once-a-week engagement that we treat as an "al la carte" system where we pick and choose what serves us best, interact with that and leave it alone. We see a program-centric entity that separates people into safe and comfortable categories where they can interact with people just like themselves and largely avoid any type of ownership or investment that will cost them anything.

Even with the focus being on a Sunday morning experience, there can be a disconnect for how the body is meant to be together. There are instances where churches separate their youth group during the message portion or have specific services for different age demographics. These are moves to alleviate any tension or temptation of boredom or distraction, but what it does is sever an arm from the body. It removes the nose and still tries to convince itself that it can smell. We convince ourselves that this system is better for everyone because it is specific instruction for people in different seasons of life, but this is not how the body of Christ works!

One of the most interesting passages in Scripture to discuss the generational disconnect between followers of God is the historical account of the Israelites rebuilding in Ezra and Nehemiah (Ezra 3). When the foundation of the new temple was built the older priests/Levites who had seen the old temple as children wept as the younger generation shouted for joy. Nobody could distinguish between the weeping and the shouts of joy. In this monumental moment in Israel's history, the younger generation lacked empathy for those who came before them, and the older generation could not be excited for what was to come in God's faithfulness. Both reactions were valid in a vacuum but when exercised together in the same space, showed the dysfunction of the Israelites at the time. The time we find ourselves in currently shows similar flaws in different ways. If the younger generation can't appreciate older traditions without being empathetic to the fear of change, while the older generation can't embrace a new direction for the body because of what once was, we are missing valuable contributions from the body. The younger and older generations need each other now, like the generations of Israel needed each other then. But instead of grappling with how to find that consensus and unity, there are plenty of instances where churches elect to separate their body into categories that seek to avoid those kinds of issues. This is driven by consumerist tendencies that are learned from living in our culture, where we'd rather spend time, energy, money, and resources to create an off-shoot ministry rather than address conflict and work through difficult components of being one body like intergenerational unity.

Our willingness to seek comfort on the altar of consumerism has led to a perversion of the organization of how the church is run, but it has also plagued the theology that is held to on a wide scale. Consumerist ideology is a breeding ground for heresy like the "Prosperity Gospel" to run rampant. It feeds the idea of the American Dream, where we have convinced ourselves that if we obey God and live our lives for Him, we will be rich, have influence, achieve success, and prosper for all of our days. Our idea of God transfigures into some type of genie who answers to every whim and pleasure that we can come up with. This transactional mentality takes over where we start believing that if we tithe and attend church every Sunday, God owes us, and we deserve to have the success the world lines out for us. The problem with operating this way is that it could not be more opposite from the truth.

43

Oftentimes, when this conversation is brought up, people are quick to quote one of their favorite verses, Jeremiah 29:11. "For I know the plans I have for you," declares the Lord, "plans to prosper you and not to harm you, plans to give you hope and a future." When this is used to describe how God's plan for our lives is only prosperity, it sounds nice. Which one of us wouldn't want only good plans in our lives? Plans that give us hope, that give us a future, that only prosper us and won't bring any harm to us? That all sounds like something we'd all sign up for. The problem is that this verse is severely taken out of context most of the time and sets believers up for failure.

Within the proper context, the Lord is giving a word through the prophet Jeremiah specifically for that time and for those people. At this point in their history, the Israelites had already been in captivity and exiled away from their home for a few years being taken by the Assyrians and then the Babylonians. Nebuchadnezzar was well into his reign as a world power and the Lord in this specific instance was comforting the Israelites that He had a plan to restore them. He fulfills that promise when Persia takes over as the next world power and releases them in Ezra/Nehemiah to rebuild their temple, wall, and eventually their city. This verse is descriptive of what was happening to Israel at that time and promises the Lord gave them to restore them to Himself after they had broken their relationship with Him by being wicked and idolatrous people. When read in the proper context, there are still positive and encouraging aspects of the historical narrative. That the Lord will restore us to Himself, even if we fall away. God will remain patient with us, always wanting us back, regardless of what we have done. His main desire is to be in a relationship with us, in a way that no false idol can ever fulfill. There is plenty in there that can give believers hope, without taking these verses out of context in a way that leads us to believe that only good things will happen in our lives if we follow Him.

The danger that resides in this type of belief, falls squarely on the fact that bad things are guaranteed to happen to us in this life. We live in a broken world, led by sin and suffering. Until Christ returns, we all will taste death. There will be sickness and pain, brokenness, and sadness. The New Testament is littered with words from Jesus, John, Paul, and Peter all outlining that there will be persecution for those who follow Him. (John 15:18; 1 Peter 3:14-17; Matthew 5:44; Luke 6:22; 1 John 3:13; 2 Timothy 3:12; etc.). If we as believers go into this life believing that only good things will happen to us and that we are promised some deformed version of the American Dream if we follow Christ, we are destined for disappointment.

The "Prosperity Gospel" feeds our consumerist tendencies. It drives capitalism and fuels society. If we subscribe to that way of thinking and we are successful, our result is making lots of money, spending lots of money, achieving worldly success, and then spending even more money. If we are prosperous, we can consume even more products that the world has to offer. These ideologies are intertwined with one another, and the world encourages us to subscribe to both. Where this breaks down is when believers encounter any kind of hardship that is guaranteed by living in a broken world. It only works when life is good, things are going your way and the world is your oyster. If something bad happens while believing the Lord only prospers you, a downward spiral ensues. The next logical step to take is that if something bad has happened, you must've done something wrong, sinned, or that the Lord is mad at you. Then begins the shame and guilt cycle that some people never recover from. It demonizes the poor and the estranged as being "less than" and elevates those who are materially wealthy. All concepts that Jesus directly contradicts in His teachings. The prosperity gospel is heresy and leads the Church into idolatrous waters, filled with the chum of consumerism. This mentality exists in every corner of the country and runs in every denomination, which is why we must collectively maintain a position of opposition to this highly destructive trend of operating.

Because we live in a society that is marked by this way of thinking, it requires intentional thoughts, actions, and habits to combat those tendencies from infiltrating the body. Leaders must constantly fight the urge to give into and appease those who want to believe in these falsehoods. But doing so will be a constant push from the norms given to us by society. Fighting these tendencies has never been harder, but there are conscientious ways for the body to battle together.

The first way the body can combat this mode of thinking is by analyzing the motives that lead to decisions. How the Sunday service is emphasized or the lack thereof. What goes on in a church service and where the focus of each component lies. Why are certain aspects of a service included or intentionally left out? Who oversees parts of the service and what purpose does it meet? How are people extrapolating what they do on Sundays into their everyday life during the week? Are certain ideologies focused on because of how they will make people feel better? Is what you are doing intentionally trying to attract more people or is it focused on teaching people how to be disciples of Christ? All decisions that are made have reasons behind them. They may not all be bad, nor do they always come from a bad place. But analyzing "why" they are made can help lead to positive conversations that help the church fight against consumerist tendencies.

An easy way to begin is by looking at and challenging the words in the worship songs we sing. Any focus on "I" and self within the songs that we sing is more focused on what we can "get" from God instead of declaring who He is. Worship is meant to be a time of exaltation, of declaration, centering oneself in who God is and what He has done. When the focus of a song leans too heavily into things "I" have done, and what "I" will do because of God, the emphasis is more consumerist and on us, which is not the point of worship. This is true of sermons as well.

What we teach and the perspective we come from matter in the lessons that are taught. Is the focus more on a humanist ideology where we are capable, we can pull ourselves up by our bootstraps, and we can change the direction of our lives? Or is it focused on the truths that reside in Scripture about who God is and what He has done? When Scripture is being taught there is a fine line between describing how the Word forms us and it being about how the Word elevates us. Yes, God loves us. Yes, when we obey Him, and He is our guide throughout life there will be things that He orchestrates that are awesome. But that doesn't mean that bad things won't happen along the way, or that the journey won't be difficult with tests, trials, and tribulations. When the Word is being taught, our focus should be on our utter dependence upon Him, His grace, mercy, and wisdom. But the onus isn't just on the pastor or those in leadership, the mentality that the rest of the body shows up with on a Sunday is just as important.

Something commonly heard among congregants after a service is something along the lines of, "it was fine, but I didn't get anything out of it" or the more spiritual version, "it just didn't feed me." When our approach to a service revolves around what we are going to get out of it, that is a clear sign that we struggle with a consumer mentality when it comes to the services we attend. Yes, should we attend, looking for things to take with us for our week? Absolutely. But if that is our only focus, and our idea of it being a successful service or not is whether we grabbed something like that for ourselves, the point of meeting together as a body is missed. To fight this type of mentality, we can intentionally think about "what can I bring"? This leads to actions during the week, as well as what we can bring on a Sunday. Who we are praying for, asking the Lord for words of encouragement for people, serving those in need, finding new people to connect with to feel welcome, etc. Typically, this type of mentality only exists with those on the payroll. But imagine a body of people whose main concern on a Sunday morning was what they could bring to others and what that would do. It creates an environment where everyone in attendance is an active participant and not just a spectator at a movie theater looking to be entertained.

The byproduct of the mentality of "what can I bring to a service" leads to a culture of investment instead of consumerism. Each person in the body has something valuable to offer others. Within each pew resides words of knowledge, words of edification and encouragement, hospitality, and administration. There are pastors and prophets, teachers, and sages. When the body congregates together, there are innumerable possibilities for how the Spirit can move among us. But that type of culture does not come naturally in a country where everything revolves around what "I" am getting out of everything. When everyone shows up, expecting to be served instead of to serve, people are bound to leave disappointed because church leaders can't uphold the impossible task of appeasing everyone's preferences. Instead of a spirit of complaining where nothing is ever good enough, everyone pitches in and invests in what is happening in the church. And weirdly enough, it is only when we give of ourselves one hundred percent to the body like this, that we experience what the Lord intended for the Church as it gathers every week.

The responsibility of taking consumerism out of our churches falls on all of us. It isn't just how leadership approaches the organization of the church, but also falls squarely on the congregants to actively participate as well. If our focus can stay in the proper place, both in and out of service, by looking for ways to invest in the body, the byproduct will be everything the book of Acts shows us is God's intention for our gathering together. Fighting consumerism and the way of the world requires all of us to set preferences in the proper place, not as a mandate but held in the palm of our hands indifferent if it is met or not. If we are meeting together as a community, striving to live like Christ did, together, around the core of orthodoxy, we should be committed to doing that life together, by investing in our local church both on Sunday morning and during the week.

Chapter 4

One Nation (Under God?)

Brick:

Why do Christians who live in the United States think that it is a "Christian nation?" Is it dangerous to view the US as "God's chosen nation?" When Christians combine their love of country and their faith, what is the result? Is the American dream part of the Gospel? Is our government holding Christian values imperative for believers to carry out their faith? What did the Early Church look like? Does it still look like that today in The United States?

Reason for analysis:

There has been an increasing amount of crossover between politics and religion in the United States. When there is a widespread belief in political leaders being "God's chosen ones" and claims that the United States is a Christian nation, that is an indicator that the lines between the two have been substantially blurred. When a nation is claimed under the moniker of being God's chosen nation, that means the fruit of the actions of that country is held under that same claim. The United States acts in many ways that do not line up with the Gospel or how the Lord operates and to associate Him with those actions is blasphemy. Claims like this are made to claim power or authority that would come from being empowered by the Creator of the Universe. This kind of power and authority is often misused and misguided in many ways, where people that are elevated within that system push their own agenda and then add the "God stamp" on top of it to justify what they are doing. It also damages the witness that Christians have in the United States when people who claim Christ are also positioning themselves for more power, influence, and the same worldly pursuits as those who don't subscribe to Christianity. Throughout history, there have been nations that have attempted to combine government and religion, and the result of that choice speaks for themselves. All Christians must understand their relationship with the government, the country they live in, their God, and the respective boxes they should fit in within their worldview.

The American Dream is not in the Gospel. The American Dream is defined as the traditional social ideals of the United States of America: Life, Liberty, and the Pursuit of Happiness. This mantra our country runs on often comes with images of "pulling yourself up by your bootstraps," getting a good job, buying a home, making a good wage, being a good consumer, saving up for retirement, retiring, and dying. None of these things are "bad" in and of themselves, but most are not biblical mandates that we are called to live by, they are just products of living in the country that we live in. To break down why the American Dream does not fit into a gospel-centric worldview, one must analyze what life, liberty, and the pursuit of happiness look like in the life of a follower of Jesus, starting with a polarizing topic in the US: liberty.

Religious freedom is something that we have as a right as a citizen within the United States, but it is not ever a guarantee that we will have religious liberties in life. In fact, a good chunk of Christians throughout history didn't and still exercised their faith anyways. Scripture never promises that we will have the freedom to follow Christ as it pertains to permission from a government, it says the opposite. We are promised to experience persecution and push back for following Christ (2 Timothy 3:11–12, John 15:19–20, Mark 10:29–30, etc.). So whatever liberties we do have in the United States, we should be thankful to have that freedom because it is not guaranteed. If people who are citizens of the United States appreciate their right to worship God, they should also stand for others to practice their own religion. It is that right that enables Christians to practice their faith, as it is with any other faith or religion. When governments get involved with who can worship what, that is where the freedom citizens have begins to go away.

Oftentimes, the American Dream infiltrates the presentation of the gospel in the form of the prosperity gospel which teaches that the way to determine if you are being righteous enough is by your material wealth and status in society. If you do not have the social ideals of life, liberty, or happiness, you must be sinning or living a life of sin. Jesus answers this question when asked about why the blind man had the impairment he had, who sinned, him or his parents, and his response in John 9:3-5: 3 was, "Neither this man nor his parents sinned," said Jesus, "but this happened so that the works of God might be displayed in him. 4 As long as it is day, we must do the work of Him who sent me. Night is coming when no one can work. 5 While I am in the world, I am the light of the world." The result of living in a broken world due to sin is that there will be things like blindness that ails humanity, this is not an indication of anything regarding someone's eternal state. Christians are called to pursue a full life, but not according to the same "signs of success" the world outlines. A believer's life should be an example of serving before receiving, loving others unconditionally, and being willing to lay their lives down for a brother/sister. That version of life is vastly different from the American life we are called to live by a society that focuses

51

on how much we can get out of this life. Focusing on how much money we make, how many material things we can acquire, how many experiences we can attain and achieve those things at any cost, even if it comes at the expense of someone else. When Christians use the word "life" it should mean something vastly different than the world using the same word, and the same is true with the word happiness.

The inherent focus of happiness is based on an individual's desires and needs. Thinking that all people should just pursue "what makes them happy" sounds great in theory, until someone's happiness coincides with someone else's, then who decides who gets to be happy and who doesn't? It is a flawed concept to believe that we can all pursue our happiness, and everything would remain equal and just. That is why believers in Christ focus on living with joy, which emphasizes taking life as it comes and finding the good in any situation which leads to peace that goes beyond understanding. Being an American citizen and living according to "life, liberty, and the pursuit of happiness" does not equal any semblance of living a gospel-centric life, which means that our main citizenship as believers is first and foremost with the King of Kings before any allegiance to the country that we live in.

The dynamic of being God's chosen nation has only been seen in history by one country and one country alone, and it isn't the United States of America. The USA is not God's chosen people/nation, nor has it ever been. In Deuteronomy 7:6 it says, "For you [Israel] are a people holy to the Lord your God. The Lord your God has chosen you out of all the peoples on the face of the earth to be his people, his treasured possession." Claims that the United States was built on Christianity are misleading because a good portion of people who signed the Declaration of Independence were freemasons, not Christ-followers. The confirmed number of freemasons that signed the Declaration is said to be eight, but twenty-four of the fifty-six signers were assumed to be. This country was not formed to be a theocracy. A theocracy is a nation where the Lord is literally their King, and everything the leader underneath the King does is from direct instructions from Him. Israel in the Old and New Testament is the only nation where God claims that role. Why does this matter? Mixing Church and State has created many issues throughout history, whether Christians were on the benefitting side, or the harmful side of that history depends on what range of history you find yourself studying - a country claiming Christianity and "acting on behalf of the faith" brings up many issues.

The best example of how this can go awry was seen during the Crusades. What started as France calling on Christians to pick up arms against Muslims to retake lands, turned into many Christians from all different nations taking up arms against Muslims and eventually Jews taking land throughout Europe and the Middle East. To convert all those people to Christianity they were offered the chance to repent and follow Christ or be murdered. Most did not choose that path, and historians outline an awful time in human history when people were murdered for not being Christian.

On the other foot, in the 20th century, Christian populations were persecuted, sometimes to the point of <u>genocide</u>, by various states, including the <u>Ottoman Empire</u>, <u>Soviet Union</u>, <u>Communist Albania</u>, <u>China</u>, and <u>North Korea</u>. They were murdered for simply being Christians and practicing their faith. Countries that bind themselves around religion or in hatred of another religion, always end poorly. Whether it is for or against Christianity, history shows us that governing based on religion does not work. The United States is not a "Christian Nation" and is not a theocracy.

If our country is inherently not Christian but is built on some Christian values, where does that leave us? In the First Amendment, it says: "Congress shall make no law respecting an establishment of religion or prohibiting the free exercise thereof" Christians are free to exercise their faith, and other people can practice their religion of choice. There has been no other nation on earth before the US that had the freedom of religion and operated as a democratic republic, we are operating differently than any other nation before us. How

Christians treat people of different faiths and beliefs matters because the world is watching.

People claim that the US is a "Christian nation," but our nation does not need to be "Christian" for believers to exercise their faith. Yes, the US holds some values that are in common with Christianity, but the US also holds values that are in common with many religions. For example, do not murder, do not steal, and do not lie, are cross-cultural/cross-religion. We have things like "One Nation under God" in our pledge of allegiance and on our money, but what does that even mean? What makes a nation "Christian"? To proclaim that one is a Christian, does not matter if your fruit does not line up with that statement. In the same way, just because people claim it to be a Christian nation, if the nation does not produce Christian fruit, how can it be considered that way?

We do not require our nation to be Christian because we do not get spiritual guidance from our government. Should we desire our nation to abide by biblical principles? Absolutely. But is it a requirement? It is not. We can influence politics by voting, advocating for our desired party, donating to campaigns, and operating within our system in America and this is not wrong and should be encouraged. But our hope can never be in a political party or political figure, period. We know that our eternal hope can only be in one place and one place alone. However, that does not preclude us from being involved in politics or affecting the culture of our nation. We are called to be in the world, but not of the world.

Lecrae said something profound as it pertains to this dynamic by saying, "What good is the gospel we preach if it doesn't reach our society? Most people in our country don't have the luxury of acting like politics don't exist. As tempting as it is for us to act like politics don't exist, the lives of real people are affected by everything we advocate for politically-our schools, our health care, our economy, equal access to the benefits of society." Although our hope is not found in our political system or a political party, we fall on a pendulum that Christians take too far one way or the other. One side is not interested or involved in politics at all, having an attitude of apathy towards our system because they know that their eternal state is secure and that is what they are looking forward to. But not having to worry about the politics of today, just means you aren't negatively affected by things that need to change. Lecrae also says, "Your perspective often depends on your proximity. Political privilege is the ability not to care about certain issues because they don't directly affect you or because you don't have categories to explain them." On the other side, are people who are too involved in politics, where they believe that if they don't have their way politically, for our nation to line up with all Christian values and beliefs, we are doomed.

Both sides are incorrect, we must live in the tension, where we care enough to be responsible citizens and to speak on behalf of those who need it, while not placing so much emphasis on the results that we lose our hope in the Lord. Having believers in politics and places of leadership is a good thing, but not an end all be all. If that isn't the case, that's the same situation as most Christians throughout history. Jesus and Paul both ran their ministry in an extremely oppressive regime with Rome. This did not stop them; in fact, it helped their cause in some ways. There has been an explosion of faith throughout China, one of the most persecuted areas of the world for believers in today's era. Obviously, we do not wish for persecution, but we should be careful about how we talk about our liberties. We should be thankful for the religious liberties we do have, but it is not a right given to us in Scripture, it is a product of living in the country that we do.

There is no persecution happening in the church within the United States currently. The churches that have been reprimanded are churches that have not obeyed the authorities above them. Romans 13 outlines that we are called to obey our authorities unless they ask us to do something that is counter to our faith, which they have not. There is actual persecution happening in China, the Middle East, and other places in the world who are being jailed, tortured, and killed for their faith, and that is not happening in the US. Our nation does not have to be led by Christians for believers to exercise our faith to the fullest.

The Church in the United States has gone mostly silent on issues that believers are mandated to lead the charge in, in many places in Scripture. And instead have been using the majority of their time and resources to fight for the cause of keeping America Christian. Not only is that a fight believers aren't called to take on, but it's also not based on fact. We should be focusing most notably on how we love each other as believers and how we love others in the world.

Genesis 9:6 describes why we should love all people, "Whoever sheds human blood, by humans shall their blood be shed; for in the image of God has God made mankind." All humans have dignity, are created in His image, and are worthy of love and respect. As Christians within the United States, we should channel our energy into loving those people because we see in Scripture what happens when followers of God don't. Israel's judgment when they overlooked injustice, exploited the poor, and forsaken the widows was severe.

Believers at large have dug their heels in, speaking out against abortion. There has even been a penchant for "All lives matter" that rings out in large gatherings of Evangelicals. Believers should operate with the perspective of all lives matter where every life is precious from womb to tomb. What fruit do we have in our lives and in our preferred political party that we see that all lives, both in the womb and outside of the womb are important? No matter their location, neither is greater than the other. All lives have value, worth, and purpose.

The Western Church in the United States has largely turned its back on those who are oppressed, who are marginalized, and who are hurting. These people who have been hurt are screaming from the rooftops about their experiences and the hurt they are experiencing, and the Church has completely missed the mark in its God-given mandate to love them the way that Christ does. The two biggest communities of people that have been the most impacted by the church's apathy are people that reside in the gay and African American communities.

As it pertains to the gay community, regardless if we think people are sinning or not, does not change our mandate to love them, to respect and treat them with dignity and honor. We all sin, and we all desire people to love us despite our weaknesses and sin. The only difference is that how they live out their choices is very public. Even within our country, there are people in the gay community that don't feel safe because of words or actions towards them from people who claim Christ as their Savior. This type of mistreatment of people is never appropriate to come from someone who follows Jesus. Unfortunately, the mistreatment outlined above is not limited to just the gay community, it also deeply impacts the African American community as well.

For a white person that sees another death of a black person in the street, it is easy to respond by saying, "but white people die too." But the difference is, is that it isn't just black people dying, it is the circumstances that they are dying in. And when they die in these painful ways, the black community doesn't just see another black person dying, they see themselves! They see their cousins, their neighbors, and their families. And when they express their communal pain, it is met with justification and platitudes, when all they want to feel is validated and cared for with actual changes that help prevent these types of deaths from happening in the future.

Somehow having discussions like this within Evangelical circles is met with accusations of attempting to be "woke," or "being a liberal and a Marxist." This isn't saying that all unrest that has come from these situations is justified and acceptable. But when did it become a partisan issue for Christians to care for the marginalized and oppressed? When we read our Bibles, what God do you see? Whether you're reading the Old or New Testament, you see a God that is a God of the oppressed! Who sees actions of injustice and takes action! **Who hears the cries of those who are marginalized, abused, and broken!** We have a group of people that are brothers and sisters in Christ, who are telling us that this is their experience and yet we do nothing! It is easier to say that it isn't happening than it is to sit in the uncomfortable reality that other believers and people have different experiences than us.

When did loving people become a partisan issue? Someone can be against abortion, and vote Democrat. Someone can be for abortion and vote Republican. It all comes down to what is the most important issue to them. You cannot dictate what is most important to others because you don't live their life, it doesn't come down to only one issue. As Lecrae said, human nature is to not care unless it impacts you directly, but it doesn't have to be that way. If a black person votes Democrat because the largest issue that matters to them falls under the categories of police brutality and unjust incarceration, that doesn't make them any less Christian, that is just what is most important to them. Any judgment of someone's salvation is sinful, that is not your place. Especially judging someone because of what political party they vote for. Neither party lines up 100% with God's Word and neither party is "God's chosen party."

Throughout Scripture, both Old Testament and New Testament, it is clear that followers of the Lord should be marked by the following: Living a life of integrity, character, truth, and love, treating all people with respect, dignity, honor, empathy, and compassion, and how you vote shouldn't change that. Being a citizen of the United States is secondary to our citizenship to the one true King.

As Christians that live in the United States, we need to repent for where we have fallen short, which isn't just asking for forgiveness, it is taking action in the opposite direction! John 13:34-35 says, "Everyone will know Christ, by how we love each other." In 1 John 4:20 the word is poignant but true when he says, "20 Whoever claims to love God yet hates a brother or sister is a liar. For whoever does not love their brother and sister, whom they have seen, cannot love God, whom they have not seen." So much of the focus of the conversation comes from those who claim Christ comes from a place of fear of losing their rights to worship the Lord which isn't in jeopardy, but in turn, have largely turned a blind eye to issues that matter like loving one another well. Those ends do not justify the means.

1 Peter 3:8-9 says, "8 Finally, all of you, be like-minded, be sympathetic, love one another, be compassionate and humble. 9 Do not repay evil with evil or insult with insult. On the contrary, repay evil with blessing, because to this you were called so that you may inherit a blessing." We are called as believers to live differently than the world, and that is supposed to be in how we love people. The United States may not be a "Christian nation," but we don't need our government to claim Christ for us to be who God called us to be. We are called to love God, love others, and be the people God created us to be.

Chapter 5

Political Alignment

Brick:

How have politics shaped the way the American church is run? Where do congregants go for direction? How involved should the Church be involved in politics? How do Americans avoid elevating their political leaders as idols in their lives? What role do politics play within the Church and in a believer's everyday life? What does 100% loyalty to a political party mean for someone's faith?

Reason for analysis:

As time has progressed in the United States, so have political power and influence come to the forefront. The 2016 and 2020 elections have shown us that politics has a way of driving a wedge between even the closest of friends and family members. Not that it has always been peaceful and tranquil in the political scene, but in the last 5 years, we've seen the political temperature of congregations turn extremely hot. To the point where congregants look to their favorite cable news source for guidance more than their local pastor. Talking points, Reddit boards, social media posts, and articles that only support an echo chamber have been dictating ideology amongst evangelicals instead of the Word of God. This phenomenon has driven people to only attend a church where the pastor will repeat and endorse cable news sound bites, and if they aren't willing to, they'll leave. This puts leadership in an extremely difficult place, knowing that if people leave, that means tithe money leaves with them, and eventually their doors close. So, we've seen many churches that support one side or another openly flourish, while pastors who are not willing to bow to one political party or the other fall on hard times. The hostility and breakdown of relationships within the Church have led many believers to abandon their local church and question why they attend a place that sounds just like the world in how it deals with politics.

The Bible very intentionally doesn't discuss specifics for how believers are to engage with their political systems. This makes sense, considering the people reading the Word since it was written are from all around the world, over many millennia, from all different countries, with their own government styles and leadership types. It would be impossible for the early church writers of the day to write something that would be easily applied to all forms of government. This is why we see in Romans 13:1-8, Paul flatly tells believers to obey the authority of the land unless it contradicts God's word:

"Let everyone be subject to the governing authorities, for there is no authority except that which God has established. The authorities that exist have been established by God. Consequently, whoever rebels against the authority is rebelling against what God has instituted, and those who do so will bring judgment on themselves. For rulers hold no terror for those who do right, but for those who do wrong. Do you want to be free from fear of the one in authority? Then do what is right and you will be commended. For the one in authority is God's servant for your good. But if you do wrong, be afraid, for

rulers do not bear the sword for no reason. They are God's servants, agents of wrath to bring punishment on the wrongdoer. Therefore, it is necessary to submit to the authorities, not only because of possible punishment but also as a matter of conscience. This is also why you pay taxes, for the authorities are God's servants, who give their full time to governing. Give to everyone what you owe them: If you owe taxes, pay taxes; if revenue, then revenue; if respect, then respect; if honor, then honor."

The system we find ourselves in, in the USA, is unique. Never has there been a country that mixes a constitutional republic and a democracy, which means even looking through history for lessons to learn from can be extremely difficult. We live in an era, where citizens of the USA are allowed the opportunity to vote for representatives, who then represent their constituents by voting for things they believe represent those who voted for them. This happens on the largest scale with the voting of the President, through the electoral college. Even though our system is vastly different from any other governmental regime in history, we are still held by the same instructions as Paul when he wrote to the Romans.

Paul's letter to the Romans was the largest letter he wrote to any one church. While in the city of Corinth around 57AD, he wrote to the church that was under the bondage of one of the most oppressive regimes in human history. At the time, Nero ruled Rome. Although it can be argued which of Rome's leaders was the cruelest, none can argue against Nero's reputation for terrible acts of violence. Nero was known for his persecution of Christians, political murders, and his exploits of sexual debauchery. Why is this important?

Within the excerpt from Romans 13, an observer could notice that Paul doesn't use any qualifiers. He doesn't say believers should obey their government only if the leader obeys God or if the country upholds Christian values, he plainly just says that we must obey. This doesn't sit well with some people because we are made aware of plenty of things we disagree with when it comes to how we are governed as a people, but that doesn't change our mandate as believers. We are a witness to the people around us when we gladly follow Christ within the constructs given to us.

With that being said, does that mean that God doesn't want us to be involved in how our country is run? Absolutely not. Inside of the constructs of how the United States is run, believers have the same right as every other citizen, which is to vote for those who represent us the best. This can and should involve the support of leaders, campaigning, empowering individuals with honesty and integrity, being informed of policies, and being a responsible citizen. Christians around the world don't have the same luxuries that believers in the USA have, but that doesn't mean it is wrong or sinful to be involved in those things. However, "how" we engage in political pursuits matters when it comes to our witness to those who don't follow Christ.

The 2020 election showed how political power and the desire to have the country be run one way over the other took precedence over the desire to be the salt and light of the world. Politicians have always hunted the Evangelical vote. Those within politics know that if they can sway Evangelicals to vote for them, they would make up a huge percentage of their constituency if they are successful. They know that if they can show support for just a few hot topics, most evangelicals would vote for them. This is where it is important to distinguish the difference between being a citizen and being a Christian. One should influence the other and not the other way around. As a citizen, we can vote for whomever we like, for any myriad of reasons. People are passionate about many different policy points that influence their voting, and it should. We as citizens of the United States should vote for whomever we deem represents us and our values the most. No person or party should be deemed the one "all Christians should vote for." The reason is that the most important topic to some is not the most important to others. Being a Christian should influence who we vote for to represent us as citizens, but who represents us should never dictate who we are as Christians.

This is where the 2020 election showed the world where American Evangelicalism stands today. Passions were inflamed, relationships destroyed, echo chambers created, and false idols firmly established. This last election brought out the worst of our humanity and showed the world that large numbers of people who claim Christ as their savior, live in fear and cling ever so tightly to false idols in the form of politicians. Representing Christ went out the window and repeating inflammatory speaking points became the norm. Whether it was in person or on social media, most people picked a side and went to battle.

Neither of the two largest parties that represent our political system in the US is Christian. Both have views that align with Scripture, and both have views that don't. People who claim to be Christians and yet aligned 100% with their party typically have their three to four reasons why the other party is way worse than theirs, but all that is whataboutism. Unfortunately, the use of whataboutism has run rampant in every corner of social media and debate, where someone can point out a valid point of concern, and because there is no good answer for it, the response typically goes something like, "Well what about... *insert something the opposite party that is also a valid point of concern*" and the conversation goes nowhere. Because of blind loyalty and whataboutism, the actions of the leaders of each party get away with practically anything with relatively no accountability from their constituents. This has created a sub-culture of Christians within each party that has taken political ideals within their party and have attempted to mesh those ideas with Christianity. Both of which in their own right, have become an adulterated heretical version of the Gospel. The two ideologies plaguing Christianity from their respective sides are "Christian Nationalism" and "Progressive Christianity."

On one side of the political spectrum, we have seen the steady rise of "Christian Nationalism." This ideology revolves around citizens of the United States who combine their love of God and love of country into a form of idolatry. When played out in practicality, this looks like the US is being elevated to the same level of importance as the Kingdom of God. Where the ends justify the means, and these citizens demand that their country be "Christian." First, a country can't be "Christian." One can only claim that title if it is a person accepting Christ. There is no such thing as Christian music, Christian nations, Christian restaurants, or anything of the sort. Can there be Christians who participate in all those areas? Of course. But to label them as "Christian" doesn't make sense. Secondly, we do not live in a theocracy, where our leaders receive divine instructions for how to run our country and God is our King. And lastly, Israel is the only country in all of Scripture that is defined as "God's chosen nation." To place The United States of America within that category is not backed up by Scripture.

What we have seen from Christian Nationalists is an alarming trend of abandoning any semblance of Christ-like behavior. The election of 2016 brought this trend to light when Evangelicals came out in large numbers to support a candidate whose living fruit is literally the opposite of what Christ teaches. Because he touted one or two important policies that matter to most Evangelicals, they were swayed into thinking that character, integrity, and Christ-like behavior didn't matter if they had power. As citizens, we have the right to vote for whomever we think would represent us the best, and those who voted for this candidate are not inherently "wrong" or "bad." But the defense of the candidate, calling him, "God's chosen one" or "The one who will save this country with God's favor" or any other titles that link God with him and his respective party is flat-out idolatry. This type of dogmatic behavior both in public and online forums became even more extreme leading up to the 2020 election.

In 2016, the support that was given to the Republican party hinged on "draining the swamp" and doing politics differently. There was merit to that thought, considering the corrupt way our government had gone about its business through the years, but the candidate they chose to represent them was morally bankrupt, abusive, harsh, and un-Christlike in almost every regard. Those who voted for him justified themselves by saying that the end justified the means. But in 2020, there was a completely different tone. Conspiracy theories abounded, false prophecies were proclaimed, and public forums were saturated with concocted narratives based on theories and hunches presented as facts. People who claim Christ as their savior were on any platform they could find emulating their candidate, engaging in fiery debate, using abusive language, and lambasting anyone who disagreed with them. We saw the rise of QaNon become prominent in these circles which enflamed conspiracy theories even further, which culminated in the insurrection of January 6th, 2021, on the Capitol in Washington D.C. where people were flying flags that claimed Christ and their devotion to their chosen leader, right next to gallows intended to murder congresspeople. The images from that day show the complete devolvement of people who claim to follow Christ but have fallen into the idolatry of Christian Nationalism. We've since seen American folk songs sung at Church, military presentations during sermons, Bibles combined with the constitution available for purchase, and more that represent this swing of public thought. This brand of Christianity is not Christian at all, it is idolatry.

Loving one's country is not sinful and, in some regards, can be commended, but when that love is elevated to inappropriate levels that equate to one's love of God or greater, that is where we can find ourselves in dangerous waters. However, it is important to note that the rise of "Christian Nationalism" partially came from a response to the direction the United States was heading in the early 2000s. With back-to-back elections that saw a Democrat being elected as President, the country began to feel the effects of a more progressive agenda. And as much as we saw people who claim Christ fall into the trap of Christian Nationalism between 2016-2020, during the time frame of 2009-2015 especially, there have been many Christians who have fallen into the trap of "Progressive Christianity."

Progressive Christianity begins and ends with the word that is in its name: Progressive. Progress in and of itself is not a bad thing, and one could argue that the constant pursuit of progress has led us to the society that we live in today. However, when combined with Christianity, progress oftentimes leads to watering down biblical truths and in extreme cases, heresy. Progressive ideologies seek to push the envelope by compromising truths that have been held since the original writing of the Old and New Testaments. This has come in many forms, that range from universalism to normalizing sin. The sinkhole that many have found themselves in, comes from a desire to marry public policy with Biblical truth.

It is incredibly important to distinguish between our role as believers and our role as citizens. There is a difference between living in a country that allows freedom of religion and extensive religious rights and compromising your faith. For example, Christians advocating for people in the LGBTQ+ community to have equal rights when it comes to healthcare, mortgages, job applications or any other right that comes from being a citizen of the United States does not indicate a compromise of their faith. As Christians, we can push for equal treatment for all citizens within the system of the United States without endorsing behavior or lifestyles while still loving people and treating them with the same dignity, respect, and honor that we are called to treat all people with. There is nuance and depth to these conversations that are oftentimes missed.

Where Progressive Christianity begins to fall off the rails, is the core desire to appease the public square by fully endorsing and encouraging agendas that are counter to what we read in Scripture. This type of move doesn't happen overnight and typically happens by adopting pieces of ideologies over time. What we consume in entertainment also leads to numbness towards certain lifestyles, actions, or language. Over time, there have been many positions held by a large majority of progressive people who claim Christ, that have been minimized or even sometimes completely removed from Church doctrine.

In Scripture, believers are called to be in the world, but not of the world (John 15:9). Those who claim Christ and abide by a more progressive worldview are prone to let go of biblical principles in exchange for ideologies that are being pushed from the world. This generally leads to a redefinition of terms, stretched interpretations of Scripture, and a more relative approach to the Word. Oftentimes, those who have fallen prey to the idolatry of progressivism pick and choose what they believe in Scripture and what they don't based on their feelings, emotions, or social movements that they identify with. When theology can be swayed based on what is currently happening in the world, that is extremely dangerous and shows where one is truly getting their guidance from.

The reality is that neither "Progressive Christianity" nor "Christian Nationalism" represent a healthy worldview for a Christian. As humans, we are drawn towards extremism and bravado, which we have in excess on both sides. Although it can be easy to begin down that road because you agree with some of their shallow points, the more you dig into each, you realize that neither represents the Gospel accurately. Following either with all your being and 100% loyalty, where nobody can even criticize valid points of concern within that party, demonstrates that your allegiance is in the wrong place.

The irony when attempting to learn more about each side is realizing how much they have in common. Both believe that someone who belongs to the opposite party could never be an "actual" Christian. They believe that if the other side were to hold dominance in the executive branch it would lead to the destruction of the country. But most of all, and the most important similarity between the two: most people from both parties just want to live their lives. At the end of the day, most people just want to live in peace, follow their dreams, drive towards their goals, be happy, live a good life, and die. People will often dismiss this truth, but the more we repeat it, the more human the "other side" becomes. We will always have more in common than we don't.

To be clear: This is not an attempt to say that one side hasn't committed horrible atrocities. Or the other side hasn't held an inhumane position or policy. It isn't saying that we as citizens should not hold our leaders accountable for wrongs they've committed or that the system we have set up doesn't need a massive overhaul. None of those things are being said. The bottom line is that divisiveness sells. In the latter half of 2021, vitriol online abated, and people discovered that the people they claimed to hate for the better half of a year, are still people that they like. This is what politics does to people who only have hope in our government to right the wrongs of this world and to have them continuously fail us. Politics thrive in polarization and extremism. When the other side can be painted as inhumane and evil, it is easy to hate them and cast distance from them. Until someone realizes that their favorite uncle claims the opposite party or your nice neighbor voted for that person that you cannot stand. It is in authentic relationships that we discover that we don't have to agree on everything to care for one another. Somehow, we have forgotten this simple truth as a nation.

It is very difficult to be 100% supportive of any one political party. Living that way is not practical for everyday life. Yes, ideologically you can hate as many people as you want and categorize all people as being "one way," but that isn't how life works. Most times, it isn't black and white. There is nuance and variables, there is personality and context. Like the premise of this book, everything derives from experiences in our lives. We have all come to the conclusions that we have and our opinions about how things should run based on our understanding that comes from firsthand knowledge. And the only way that these experiences and nuance can be understood is through empathy and relationship.

Separation from relationships and fear-mongering is the easiest way to divide people. This isn't a new concept, even Jesus says, "And if a house be divided against itself, that house cannot stand." When he is discussing why He couldn't cast out demons if he was Satan as he was being accused of. When we engage in relationships with one another, when we pray for one another, care about the wounds each of us has and invest in relationships, the less scary we become towards one another. As believers, our life's mission is to be the salt and light of the earth. Because we don't have to wait until we die to begin eternity, we can see our lives here on earth as eternity, because we have a relationship with Christ. This means, how we live this life matters.

In Jeremiah 7, Jeremiah is speaking on behalf of the Lord as a prophet, warning the people of Judah and Jerusalem what kind of wrath is going to be exercised on them because of their disobedience and worship of false idols. Within these passages, the Lord describes how they can avoid His wrath and explains why what they are doing is wicked:

> *"This is the word that came to Jeremiah from the Lord: Stand at the gate of the Lord's house and there proclaim this message: 'Hear the word of the Lord, all you people of Judah who come through these gates to worship the Lord. This is what the Lord Almighty, the God of Israel, says: Reform your ways and your actions, and I will let you live in this place. Do not trust in deceptive words and say, "This is the temple of the Lord, the temple of the Lord, the temple of the Lord!" If you really change your ways and your actions and deal with each other justly, if you do not oppress the alien, the father, or the widow and do not shed innocent blood in this place, and if you do not follow other gods to your own harm, then I will let you live in this place, in the land I gave your forefathers for ever and ever. But look, you are trusting in deceptive words that are worthless."* - Jeremiah 7:1-8*

The people of Israel were claiming that they acknowledged God and His temple. They said a lot of the right things, but their actions were in direct contrast to those words. There has been a lot of talk in modern times about what the focus of believers should be when it comes to politics. What topics Christians should care about most and what God really cares about. He lines it out bluntly in verse 5 when He says, *"If you really change your ways and actions and <u>deal with each other justly</u>, if you <u>do not oppress the alien</u>, the <u>fatherless</u> or the <u>widow</u> and <u>do not shed innocent blood</u> in this place, and if you <u>do not follow other gods</u> to your own harm."*

Within these passages, we see clearly that God is not just interested in the words that come out of our mouths, but also the heart in which we say them, and the actions that back them up. God's desire for His people that comes from Jeremiah can be directly applied to all Christians now, because it is demonstrating the heart that He desires for His people. The principles remain the same. When we are engaged in politics, the things that should matter to us most as lined out in Jeremiah 7, are focusing on justice, extinguishing oppression, aiding those who cannot help themselves, not killing or harming innocent people, and not worshiping any false idols (which include people). If our actions line up with the list given to us in Jeremiah 7, we can be rest assured that we are supporting what we are called to support.

It is not a requirement that our government leads from a Christian perspective. As believers, do we want our government to line up with our values? Absolutely. But it is not mandated that our government do our bidding as Christians for us to live out the full extent of what God is calling us to live.

Engaging in politics as a believer is tough. We believe in the sovereignty of Christ, but we also have the opportunity to influence elections through voting, campaigning, and advocating for the candidates we believe will best represent us. We must keep politics in the correct box when evaluating the things that are important to us. Depending on politics to save us or believing that solving some problem in the government is going to bring any kind of salvation is idolatry, but we also need to be responsible citizens and engage within the system to bring about change that God has placed on our hearts. Again, this is not binary, there are no simple solutions.

How we align ourselves politically, is going to be grounded in our experience. It is not our place, nor our responsibility to make others think like ourselves. We need to focus on all the things we have in common, not the things we differ on. I heard it said once, "Everyone has their calling, pursue yours." It was said within the context of a conversation, where it was expressed, that people get frustrated when someone isn't as passionate about an important topic as they are. The reason why is because you are called to be passionate about that topic to bring about change, and other people are called to be passionate about others to bring about change in those areas.

Politics are important, but they should never be elevated as an idol in our lives, where we fight to the death because it is an "end all, be all." It can be extremely easy to elevate politicians as idols in our lives because we believe that they can bring about change that we think is necessary to live a better life. But the reality is that no change happens outside of God's will. As Christians, how we engage in politics is a witness to our country and the world. Stand for what we are called to stand for, and let the rest take care of itself.

Chapter 6

Race

Brick:

How do racial divisions affect the church? What does it look like to achieve racial reconciliation? Is the church meant to be multicultural? How does the church approach racial conversations prevalent in US culture? Why does the church need to address the issue of race?

Reason for analysis:

The issue of race has a long and complicated history, especially in the United States. Because this is an issue that drives to the depth of humanity and how it affects how people engage in everyday life in this country, it also impacts the church. Oftentimes it is easier for the Church to avoid such difficult topics to tackle, but that has led to complicate matters further. The treatment of all people is a deeply Gospel-centric issue that has a direct impact on all of humanity being created in God's image. If that is true and all of humanity are image-bearers, that means any topic that threatens the sanctity of that truth must be confronted. Some systems exist both in and outside of the Church in the US that are desperately in need of restoration, reconciliation, and healing. When believers analyze this brick in their worldview, it can be easy to become defensive and choose to not engage. If this continues to be an issue in the modern-day church in the US, the Church will remain in a constant state of deficiency.

Understanding racism through the lens of Scripture is difficult. Mainly because in Scripture we don't see instances of people being hated because of the color of their skin, but rather what country they come from or what class they belong to. There are many aspects of this hatred that we do see that have parallels to racism, but there aren't any examples in Scripture that someone was solely hated because of the color of their skin. This creates a situation where one needs to distill down similar principles that we can find in Scripture and apply them to modern-day issues.

The parable of the Good Samaritan in Luke 10:25-37 is an appropriate place to start. It is a good thought exercise to insert oneself into the parable and ponder which person you'd be. Simply put, the parable is an instance that Jesus portrays, where a man was attacked by robbers and left to die. Multiple people passed by him, including a priest and a Levite, but it wasn't until a Samaritan saw him that the man was tended to. The Samaritan used his resources (bandages, oil, and wine), placed the injured man on his donkey, and took care of him in an inn. When the Samaritan left the inn, he left money for the stay and advocated for the injured man by asking the innkeeper to look after him.

Jesus telling this parable and using the specific people He used was intentional. The priests and Levites represented a higher class within that society, while the Samaritans were viewed as no higher than dogs at that time. So, for Jesus to use them as an example of how He is calling all people to love others, He is showing them that class or social status should not impact how we love and help others.

If you've ever wondered which person you'd be in that parable, how you engage the issue of a race right now in today's climate indicates that quite clearly. Regardless of your class or status, we have people in our congregations that are communicating that they are injured, have been attacked, struggling, and left half dead either physically, emotionally, or spiritually, and how you've responded is a direct indication of how you'd respond in the parable of the good Samaritan. It isn't the role of the person walking by to determine how hurt someone is or if they were deserving of being attacked, Jesus shows us that it is our job as followers of Him to heal, love, restore and empower healing through any means we have necessary. But as the Levite and the Priest show us, they saw the man and chose to ignore his plight by not just walking by him, but by intentionally walking on the other side of the road.

Acknowledging that there is an issue, is the first step in achieving any kind of resolution. The not-so "elephant in the room" is that there is racial tension in our culture, but we would be remiss to think that tension doesn't also exist in our churches. This breakdown begins and ends with a lack of empathy. There have been countless brothers and sisters in Christ telling the church in the US that they have experienced racism in many forms within their walls. When this very sensitive conversation occurs, the individual receiving that information has two choices:

1. Believe them, listen to their personal experiences, sit in the uncomfortable truth that there are things to work on, and engage them.

2. Explain how what they experienced wasn't racism, but a product of something else, or it was imagined, deflect any responsibility, and continue operating as though nothing happened.

The reason why these problems all boil down to empathy is that if those in leadership can't truly hear the people experiencing these situations and put themselves in their shoes, there will never be enough urgency to actually make any changes. If the listener's point of view is that there aren't any versions of racism that they've seen, it is easier to dismiss the entire topic. Actively listening to the person describing their experiences is the first step necessary to understanding. There is a reason why we as humans find other people's stories so captivating. The reason is that their experiences are far different from our own. We don't have a hard time believing people's stories when they aren't politically charged, but especially in today's climate, the stories that are being shared by people who have encountered these situations in the church are largely ignored or explained away.

Most of the time, when these stories are shared, the person describing what has happened to them is not looking for anything other than validation and for the recipient to hear them. Listening without getting defensive leads to empathy. Engaging with the difficult paradigm that friends, congregants, and neighbors have had a different experience than you can be jarring at first. But just like any case of trauma or pain, having someone just listen without fear of judgment or retaliation is the first step to healing.

Whether you think racial issues are real or not, or if you are engaged in them is irrelevant. When people are telling you that they have experienced very real instances of racism within your walls, as a responsible leader, you must listen. If there was any other form of discrimination or harm being done, leadership is quick to intervene, and issues of race should be no different.

Once it has been established that there are not only racial tensions, but there are serious cracks in the foundation of how the church engages with racial issues, a genuine conversation about where those cracks are can begin. Most of the problems that are brought up tend to be a product of broken-down systems and "church as we've always done it." It can be difficult to hear when you can point to many other churches in the area or your past that have always done it a certain way which has not been described as racially insensitive before.

This conversation can oftentimes fall on deaf ears because practical examples aren't always easy to describe, nor solutions readily offered. It is not the role of the hurt congregant to solve racial disparities in their church. To engage with this topic and toil with what the application looks like, is going to be individual to each church or denomination, but there are a few common instances that are widespread in many churches in the US that are a good place to start. The issues brought up below came from a process of relationship, conversations, hearing, observing, and taking notes from multiple sources. Three starting points that can help begin the conversation about addressing racial disparities in the church are tokenism, toxic charity, and stylistic separation.

Avoiding tokenism within the operation of a church can be difficult. But if there is a conversation about "increasing diversity" and the result from that conversation ends with asking a certain congregant of color to just "do the announcements," it's something worth addressing. Making the church appear more diverse without giving any people of color a place at the table, is not authentic diversity. The leadership within a church should represent its body, and that body should represent the community that the church is in. If including a person of color in marketing material for an outreach event is more of a strategic move to attract more people of color, without that same representation in leadership, that is another form of tokenism.

The challenge that resides within tokenism, is that most of the time it comes from good intentions. It isn't always the case, but when the mic is given to someone of color, it can feel like the "diversity" box has been checked. But doing menial tasks for the sake of appearance is a crack in the foundation of many churches. Even though the intention may be to give a person of color stage time to show congregants that there are people of color in your church, that blip of stage time doesn't deter anyone from noticing the lack of representation within leadership. Using people of color to portray realities that don't exist is doing more harm than good. The answer isn't to stop having people of color on stage, it is to give them a voice and the ability to speak in the direction of the church and how to engage people from all walks of life.

How the church engages with its community and hosts events has historically been a blind spot for churches. Oftentimes, churches in the US are happy to give of their resources and time, if they can do what they want to do and serve how they want to serve on their terms. What this has led to is many instances of churches running outreaches that they've "always" run, or leadership has come up with but leads to further dependence on future ministries. This is also known as "toxic charity." When churches focus on bringing what they deem is best for a community and leave the people they are serving out of the conversation, that can lead to further fracturing within the church's foundation. Two places that the church in the US sees this type of charity most predominately are on short-term mission trips and community service projects.

Again, these types of events in and of themselves are not bad, sinful, or wrong, but how the church goes about putting them on has drifted into toxic charity at times. When short-term mission trips or community service projects are more focused on what the individuals who are going on the trip or putting on the project get out of it, and not on the people they are serving, priorities are misplaced.

Take a prototypical short-term mission trip:
- Church decides to go on a short-term mission trip
- Church then decides which city/town/country that said mission trip is going to
- Church decides who is going on the mission trip
- Church decides what the people who are going on the mission trip are going to do
  - This generally revolves around VBS, random service projects like painting something, doing yard work, etc.
- Church decides the amount of money to donate and materials to be given to the church where they are going
- Church sends their mission team, pictures are taken, "vacation" days are added on either side of the trip, experiences are had,

and those who attended had their "eyes opened" so they don't take their lives for granted.

- The mission team goes home and reports back what happened on the trip so the church feels like their investment from tithes/offering was worth it.

- The church that they went to, now has the resources that were given to them that are finite and only last a short time. They return to the normalcy of life they had previously until the next mission team comes in.

Someone may read this list and exclaim, "There are some good things that are happening in that list," to which I would agree! Again, issues like this are not black and white, they are not binary 1's and 0's. There is nuance and understanding that needs to come from a different point of view. In the example listed above, multiple elements lead to this type of charity being "toxic."

The church that is receiving the charity oftentimes must come up with service projects for the missionaries to do while they are there. Most of the time, these projects are not needs, but just things for the missionaries to do to fill their time. Their actual needs go unmet and things that would help them build in a direction that didn't make them depend on missionary groups remain.

1. The mission team leaves the people they are coming to serve no better than when they came. They may have solved a few temporary problems, but those problems reappear the second those finite resources dry up.

2. Temporary relationships are built, especially with children, mission trip attendees take pictures with them for their social media, claim they will be in a relationship with them forever, and then return home back to their comforts leading to confusion from the people they came to serve. After a short time, those passions fade, life gets busy, and those relationships are forgotten. Imagine this happening multiple times a year to the same kids/people over and over and over again.

3. If the trip has a vacation/sightseeing day built in and that is what is advertised to get people to go on the trip, what is the real motive behind going? What does that communicate to the people the trip is supposed to serve?

4. The church sending the missionaries are the ones dictating who goes, what resources they bring, what happens, how they build an "experience" for those who go, how they serve, when they need meals, etc., and basically every other aspect of the time they spend in that place. In turn, the results of the trip only benefit those who go and the experience they were able to have.

Reading this breakdown of short-term mission trips may bring up the question of why toxic charity is being addressed in the chapter written about race. When attempting to solve tensions that arise from race, oftentimes churches will take the same approach with toxic charity. Where the church will decide for people of color what they are going to do to "make things right" without even talking to them or inviting them to sit at the table. The church's idea of reconciliation is based on what they are prepared to do, instead of asking what they should be doing that would lead to actual impact. What happens frequently in churches, is they will start the process of attempting to heal racial wounds with good intentions but go about it in ways that aren't as effective as they could be.

It may not be in the form of a mission trip, but how the church puts on outreach and community events follow similar patterns. The church decides what they would like to do, raise the resources to do it, tell the community they are serving what they are prepared to do, come in and do it, and the results are the same as the second list above. This is a pattern of toxic charity that falls under the category of "how the church has always done it," especially in the last 20-30 years. When outreach is focused on how it benefits the missionary/congregant more than how it empowers the people that are supposed to be the benefactors of these events, there is a massive disconnect. The goal of these outreach events, as spoken from the stage, is to bring people from the community into the church putting them on. But is the church a place where people from the community would want to come and feel welcome?

A trend that has emerged in the evangelical church in the United States, is one of intentional separation based on race. Where you can drive down a road and see a church that is in the name designated as a "Korean" church or "AME" church that identifies itself by the predominant race of the people who attend. These churches began largely because of treatment that they received within the walls of mainstream denominations. It isn't wrong or sinful to congregate in this way but the splintering of churches based on race prevents the Church from being the fully expressed multi-ethnic, multi-cultural meeting place it is meant to be. Because of this trend, it became easy for people to choose their church based on stylistic differences and preferences. It is much easier to do things how it has always been done than to integrate cultural backgrounds and experiences.

The failure of churches to appropriately integrate different cultures and expressions into church services has led to another crack in the foundation of "how we do church." In Galatians 3:26-29, it says, "So in Christ Jesus, you are all children of God through faith, for all of you who were baptized into Christ have clothed yourselves with Christ. There is neither Jew nor Gentile, neither slave nor free, nor is there male and female, for you are all one in Christ Jesus. If you belong to Christ, then you are Abraham's seed, and heirs according to the promise." Paul, when speaking to Galatia isn't saying that there will no longer be distinctions between us, he is saying that who we are as one body is of far greater importance. This means that integration and multicultural expressions of our faith are what the design of the body is supposed to look like. Where cultural expressions of faith are celebrated, taught, and encouraged in a blend that doesn't elevate one over the other. Part of what leads to the racial divide within our congregations is our unwillingness to adapt to a multicultural expression of faith. The body has gotten so used to separating itself based on race, that it would require an intentionally focused effort of meeting together as one body to resolve this breakdown.

The process of achieving racial reconciliation starts with empowerment and partnership. Part of our call as believers is to empower one another. Giving isn't just monetary, it is our time, our resources, our expertise, and anything that we can give to the body. What would it look like to talk with the local leaders, asking what their biggest need is in the community and filling that with the resources we have? Rather than coming in, telling them what we are going to do, building an "experience" for those that attend, but giving no long-term betterment to the community we are serving. What would it look like to build a mission team around the needs of the church the trip aims to serve, instead of building an experience for the needs of the missionaries? Pastor says that local businessmen need entrepreneurial advice to help sustain their business and how to be Christ-followers in a secular work environment. Imagine the church filling that need with people of their congregation who are successful Christian businesspeople going, running a leadership seminar with one-on-one training, and providing long-term solutions to help them be successful in business and more effective in their ministry to people through it. That kind of help leads to empowerment and partnership instead of one-sided toxic charity. The result is the missionary fills a tangible need, the church is empowered, Christ is amplified, and the impact is long-lasting and effective. Partnership and empowerment require supernatural empathy. To truly hear what someone else's experience is, to empathize and put yourself in their shoes, and not show pity or feel sorry for them but empower them and help give them resources to become a true partner.

This is the case with minority members of your church and community. Instead of seeing a reconciliation as a handout, what if the church saw that as an opportunity to empower and build people up? Where is the church equipping people in their church and community with tools, assets, and resources that help them in tangible and long-term ways? Analyzing what Scripture has to say about the power of resources, the "Rich Young Ruler" in Matthew 19:16-30 shows the reader a man who has claimed to give everything to the Kingdom, so Jesus tells him to lay down his riches and come follow Him. The man declines. When reading this passage, it can be easy to think that the man was just stingy with his money. But that isn't the case. It was the man's means and resources that he was unwilling to part with. As the body of Christ, we freely hold our hands open because everything we have has been given to us. This is not just limited to money. This is our time, our energy, our resources, and our connections. How we can serve our community has endless possibilities if we are willing to give whatever is required of us. The problem is that these methods can't be listed in a book because what a community needs is going to be dependent on the community. And the only way to gain that information is to bring someone to the table that is from the community and allow them to shape what that looks like.

A powerful means of empowering people is giving them a say, asking for their advice, and giving them a seat at the table to influence what decisions are made. This doesn't mean giving someone the right to dictate a new way of doing things by themselves, it means being at the table where decisions are made by the church for how they go about their business-like outreaches, trips, and engagement in the community. Representation is a cornerstone in creating a healthy church environment where people from the community know that their needs are being heard and met by leadership. When there is representation present within church leadership that also brings a voice towards embracing a multicultural reality.

Embracing someone else's culture is always an intentional choice. The culture that we preside in naturally is where we are going to feel the most comfortable. And human nature dictates that we are always going to prefer being in our comfort zone over any other option, which means we must choose to go outside of it. Pursuing a multicultural and multiethnic community within a church requires commitment, patience, and most importantly the ability to build relationships with all people from all backgrounds and ethnicities. When the people in a congregation feel represented, that their culture is celebrated and accepted and they are empowered to live the life God has called them to live, that is where a healthy multicultural reality resides.

Confronting the issues that come with racial division is going to be messy. They aren't easy to address, and it requires persistence. This type of reconciliation isn't flashy. It isn't social media worthy. It requires genuine effort, investment, relationship, listening, and the most difficult: time. Once the church in the United States can come to terms with the racial issues that it has, truly listens, and addresses breakdowns that reside in the foundation of the church, there we can begin healing, restoring, and reconciling what is broken. What was presented in this chapter is not the full extent of issues that need to be addressed, but it is a tangible starting point to begin the conversation and challenge us to be the ones to stop on the road and take action to assist and empower brothers and sisters in Christ who have experienced racially-based pain in the church.

Chapter 7

The Leadership of Women

Brick:

What do we see in churches in the US today regarding women? What roles do they have? How are they limited? Viewed? Discussed? How does the Bible talk about women? Should women have "lesser" authority or only work with other women and children? Does a woman have the ability to teach or preach?

Reason for analysis:

Depending on the denomination that one belongs to, the views on women in leadership within the Church vary. There is an almost daily discourse on social media and even outrage towards certain women that are more prominent because of ministries they have led and books they have written. How the Church constructs its leadership is incredibly important and should be done in such a way that represents the community of people they choose to serve. This issue is a constant friction point among evangelicals, which is why this brick should be investigated and analyzed thoroughly to understand God's desire for women within the context of church ministry.

To look at this issue properly, we cannot just look at one or two verses to guide our perspective. It is important to see what is said in those verses in the context of the entire Bible and see how God treats women, the roles they did or didn't play, and analyze His interactions with them to see how He views them. Observing the historical accounts of women throughout Scripture, especially instances where women played a significant role, should provide the reader with a holistic perspective that will apply to roles that women can or should hold in today's era of the Church.

There is a myriad of moments in both the Old and New Testaments that demonstrate the many roles that women have held throughout history. Listed below are a handful of women who had prominent noteworthy events transpire in their lives that were important enough for the writers of each book to mention. It is important to view these instances on both their individual and collective merit. Each outline both the importance of the specific call on each woman's life and shows God's mindset towards the role of women in general.

Women who witnessed the resurrected Christ and communicated the first version of what we now consider "The Good News:" Mary Magdalene, Mary (mother of Jesus), Mary (wife of Clopas) - Matthew 28:1-10; Mark 15:47-16:8; John 20:10-18; Luke 23:55-24:12

None of the Gospel writers were present when Jesus made His first appearance after the resurrection and there is debate about who was there and when. But one thing is unanimous in all accounts, that the first witnesses of the resurrected Christ were women. Whether it was directly speaking to Jesus first, or angels and then Jesus, or just angels, these women were charged with telling the disciples the news that Jesus had defeated death and was exactly who He claimed to be.

The most important message in human history was spoken to and entrusted to women to communicate to the world. All three Marys were close to Jesus throughout His ministry and had varying influences on His life. This honor, of being the first to see the resurrected Christ and then also given the task to go and share that news with the disciples is arguably one of the most monumental moments in all of Scripture.

Deborah - Judges 4 & 5

It is well documented throughout Israel's history in the Old Testament that God appointed leaders within Israel, both Kings and Judges. Some proved wicked, some proved righteous. After the death of Ehud, Deborah was appointed the Judge of Israel. She was married to Lappidoth and is described as a prophetess and judge over all of Israel. Her position is in no way intertwined with her husband or his credentials, he is merely a footnote. God Himself designated her as the Judge of Israel and is recognized as a prophetess within the Old Testament.

The role of "prophet" is simply defined as someone who speaks on behalf of God. This is not limited to only speaking of what is to come. There are many cases throughout Scripture where prophets speak words of comfort, encouragement, calls of repentance, and desire for reconciliation that have nothing to do with the future. All people in the Bible that are deemed prophets or prophetesses are the mouthpieces of God Himself. Deborah taught and spoke words of admonishment and encouragement which led to moves of God within the Israelites and filled the responsibilities that aligned with being a prophetess.

Deborah was also a judge. Before the time of Kings, God utilized Judges to rule Israel. These individuals oversaw leading Israel, commanding the military, dealing with issues that arose, and imposed consequences on people who did not obey the Lord's will within the theocracy. This position was the highest power within Israel at the time and saw many different leaders hold that rank before Israel cried out for a human king. These chosen few were entrusted with the care of Israel, to lead and to guide, to punish and reward and most importantly impose God's will through His people.

Rahab - Joshua 2:9-13

The account of Rahab is well known among believers. All it took for her to boldly disobey the King of Jericho and assist the spies that she was housing was to simply hear about Israel and the God that was for them. This was a woman of ill-repute, being a prostitute, and yet the Lord still empowered her to help Israel take over the Promised Land.

Exemplifying boldness, courage, and profound trust, Rahab wasn't asked to do the things she did for the spies, it was her idea. By taking the action that she did, the spies' lives were spared, and Joshua was given the confidence needed to march the Israelites around Jericho's walls and ultimately take over the city in their conquest of Canaan.

That would be enough to acclaim her and record her name in the history of Israel. But God took it another step further. In Matthew 1:5, Rahab is listed in the genealogy of Christ. Once the Israelites took over Jericho and her family was spared, Rahab married Salmon (of Judah) and became the mother of Boaz. Not only did she heroically bring Israel to victory, but she is also a matriarch in a long list of God's chosen people that led to Christ's birth. The honor bestowed on a once prostitute shows God's profound desire for redemption among us all and demonstrates that even if a woman is destitute in the eyes of the world, the Lord can still redeem and empower her to do mighty things in the name of the Lord.

Esther - Esther 1-10

Coming from a unique perspective, Esther came from a place of prominence and power. However, she was not born into it. Living as a Jew under a foreign King's rule and after her parents died when she was young, Esther was an orphan with no future ahead of her, or so the world would have thought. The disobedience of Queen Vashti led to King Xerxes taking away her position and giving it to someone else. When looking for his next Queen, King Xerxes sent out a search party only using beauty as the measure for him to decide on his next bride. Esther was chosen because of her beauty, but Xerxes quickly discovered that Esther was a woman of confidence, honor, character, and integrity.

Because of her position within the kingdom, it would have been easy for her to ignore the issues of her people that were struggling. But she didn't. There were two major instances where Esther could have remained quiet, and she would not be affected at all. However, she did what was right and what needed to be done.

The first of which was when she reported the assassination attempt that Mordecai overheard which turned out to be true. This moment of obedience gave her credibility in the eyes of the King and ended up being the reason why the King would hear her a second time. Haman had deceived the King into providing an edict demanding the murder of all Jews because Mordecai wouldn't bow before him. Esther hadn't been in the King's presence in over 30 days and was only supposed to be in his presence if he called for her. It was a huge risk for her to approach him with something that she wanted to address with him without an invitation.

The consequence of approaching the King without him calling for her was death. But the lives of her people were on the line, and she knew she had to do what was right, regardless of what would come next. Esther showed boldness, selflessness, courage, assertiveness, and resolve by approaching the King and eventually saving her people from destruction. It was her action, that only she could have taken, that saved her people.

Naomi & Ruth - Ruth

By all standards of her time, Naomi was "past her prime" and seen as a "burden of the state" because she was a widow. Widows were seen in the same light as disabled and homeless people at the time. As far as society at that time was concerned, those people did not have much worth associated with them. Even though society saw her that way, she still chose to encourage Ruth, guide her on her path, and give her advice on how Ruth could be the woman of God that she was called to be, one of honor and noble character. God empowered Naomi regardless of her age and gave her the boldness to play her part in the development of younger women around her.

Ruth by her own volition also showed godly traits by loving Naomi above and beyond what was required of her. By staying with Naomi, she intentionally chose not to further herself, but to assist a woman that had lost both her husband and her sons. This character, one who puts others' needs above her own and carries herself in an honorable way, demonstrates a life after the heart of God. This type of commitment to a life of character and honor led to her being a part of the lineage of David after marrying Boaz, which led to the birth of Christ.

Priscilla - Romans 16:3-4

Priscilla and Aquila were known missionaries of the time and Paul commends them for the work they had done with the Gentile churches in Rome. Paul intentionally lists Priscilla first and she is also mentioned first in Acts 18:24-28 when Luke writes about the couple. To list them this way is very uncommon and insinuates that Priscilla was the main contributor to the movement that Paul and Luke are referencing. She had a calling placed on her life that the Lord empowered within her to be a voice of truth among new believers in the house church that she led.

"There are some scholars that believe that Priscilla was actually the writer of the book of Hebrews. The book is not claimed by any of the disciples and most authors name themselves at the beginning of their writings. It is a possibility that because she was a woman, the letter would not be distributed because of cultural antagonism towards women during that era. Being nameless, the letter would be read based on the merits of the content and not who wrote it, so it is possible that she wrote it but we may never know."[1]

As a missionary to the churches in Rome, Priscilla engaged in teaching, preaching, guiding, and encouraging believers. Within Acts, Luke describes a situation where Apollos was teaching an incomplete version of the gospel, so Priscilla and Aquila take him back to their house to explain the way of God more adequately. Not only do we read about Priscilla being a noteworthy missionary from the perspective of Paul, but we also see her training and correcting a man who was learned and instructed in the ways of the Lord. There is no indication from what was written that how Priscilla was leading was wrong in the eyes of the people in the early Church made up of both men and women.

Phoebe - Romans 16:1-2

Phoebe was known as a deaconess of the Church in Cenchrea. In Romans, Paul lets the Church in Rome know that she was being sent to them to help build the church there. The role of deacons/deaconesses in the Church of the New Testament can be described as "lay work." This is where the deacon or deaconess helps with the tangible needs of the local church. These needs can vary and typically consist of them taking care of logistical needs, supporting other church leadership, facilitating helping the poor, the widows and sick, and basically any other logistical need the church had.

Many theologians believe that Phoebe was the one to deliver the letter from Paul to the Church of Rome. This is evident by the language that Paul references to Phoebe and his instructions to receive her well, take care of her needs, and allow her to continue her ministry within the Roman body of believers. The same language is used when Paul sends other missionaries to other cities and Paul makes sure that the churches knew that it was he that sent them and instructs them to take care of the missionaries when they arrive. It is

---

[1] Hoppin, Ruth. *Priscilla's Letter: Finding the Author of the Epistle to the Hebrews.* Lost Coast Press, 2000

noteworthy that Paul empowered Phoebe to not only be sent on a mission to Rome but also tasked her to be the one to deliver the letter. This shows how Paul views Phoebe and her contributions to the gospel being spread and the development of local churches as extremely valuable.

These historical accounts establish that women are present in some of the Bible's most powerful moments in history and played monumental roles within them. They are placed in the middle of some of the most noteworthy moments that Christians revere and are asked to use their specific talents, giftings, and callings to contribute to them in powerful ways. After analyzing the breadth of women's influence throughout the Old and New Testament, the logical next step is to break down the verses that have led to the doctrinal positions held by most evangelical churches in the United States in the 21st century.

Where does this doctrine come from? There are two passages that most people point to when they want to discuss a woman's role in the church and otherwise:

1 Timothy 2:11-15:

"A woman should learn in quietness and full submission. I do not permit a woman to teach or to have authority over a man; she must be silent. For Adam was formed first, then Eve. And Adam was not the one deceived; it was the woman who was deceived and became a sinner. But women will be saved through childbearing-if they continue in faith, love, and holiness with propriety."

Ephesians 5:22-24:

"Wives, submit to your husbands as to the Lord. For the husband is the head of the wife as Christ is the head of the church, his body, of which he is the Savior. Now as the church submits to Christ so also wives should submit to their husbands in everything."

Breaking down the context and other biblical references within these passages can help us understand what Paul was emphasizing through these verses. Within the analysis earlier in this chapter, it is apparent that Paul had a great deal of trust and belief in women like Priscilla and Phoebe and empowered them within their respective ministries. How does this fit with the things he is teaching to Timothy and the church in Ephesus?

1 Timothy:

The background of the book of 1 Timothy is important to consider when reading and interpreting what Paul is driving at as it pertains to a woman's role within the church. Within the book, Paul is instructing Timothy on how he should construct the gathering of believers that he was entrusted to pastor. Breaking down chapter 2, Paul outlines details of what an orderly worship service should look like and discusses the same emphasis in other letters he wrote as well. To fully understand what he is referencing when discussing a woman's role in the church, we must investigate the context to gain a full understanding of his intent.

1 Timothy 2:

"I urge, then, first of all, that requests, prayers, intercession, and thanksgiving be made for everyone, for kings and all those in authority, that we may live peaceful and quiet lives in all godliness and holiness. This is good and pleases God our Savior, who wants all men to be saved and to come to a *knowledge of the truth*. For there is one God and one mediator between God and men, the man Christ Jesus, who gave Himself as a ransom for all men-the testimony given in its proper time. And for this purpose I was appointed a herald and an apostle-*I am telling the truth, I am not lying-and a teacher of the true faith to the Gentiles*. I want men everywhere to lift holy hands in prayer, without anger or disputing. I also want women to dress modestly, with decency and propriety, not with braided hair or gold or pearls or expensive clothes, but with good deeds, appropriate for women who profess to worship God. A woman should *learn* in quietness and full submission. I do not permit a woman to *teach* or to have authority over a man; she must be silent. For Adam was formed first, then Eve. And Adam was not the one *deceived*; it was the woman who was *deceived* and became a sinner. But women will be saved through childbearing-if they continue in faith, love, and holiness with propriety."

There is a common theme that is interwoven throughout chapter 2 which illuminates what Paul's main point is through these verses. Paul emphasizes that all people (men being used as a "catch-all" like Americans say "guys" when referencing both men and women) when they are saved need to come to a "knowledge of the truth." He then references a few sentences later that he is an example of someone teaching the truth and exemplifying true faith to non-Jewish people (i.e., Gentiles). He goes on to describe how men are to behave within a church setting and how women should present themselves with decency by dressing modestly and performing good deeds. At this point, Paul uses women as an example.

After describing the knowledge of the truth that is required and describing himself as a teacher of the faith to the Gentiles, he brings up women. He then outlines that women should not teach and should learn in quietness and full submission, all while being silent. This is strange because we see in the case of Priscilla, that she not only taught the word but also led a small house church in her home. Paul lauds her abilities and makes a note to mention her in the book of Romans. This is peculiar considering in 1 Timothy it seems like he is saying that women should not teach. So, then what is Paul saying?

While writing, Paul often breaks things down in a way not too different from a lawyer (which comes as no surprise considering his background as a Pharisee). He makes a point and then uses evidence or examples to prove his point. 1 Timothy 2 is a perfect example of this. Paul describes what he views as an effective teacher of the word, and then uses women as an example of people who would not be an effective teacher of the word. But why are women used as an example of someone who would not be a good teacher in that era?

Paul uses Adam and Eve, as an illustration, to drive the point home about something extremely important when it comes to a leader teaching the Word to the congregation: *that person should not be easily deceived*. He points out that Adam was created first, then Eve, and that it was in fact Eve who was deceived by the serpent, not Adam. To understand his illustration, we must read the account for ourselves to see what he is referencing, which can be found in Genesis 2.

Genesis 2:15-17

"The Lord God *took the man* and put him in the Garden of Eden to work it and take care of it. And the Lord God *commanded the man*, "You are free to eat from any tree in the garden; but you must not eat from the tree of knowledge of good and evil, for when you eat of it you will surely die."

Something to notice here is that God commanded Adam. Not Adam and Eve, just Adam. Continuing, we see that God then creates Eve.

Genesis 2:18-22

"The Lord God said, "It is not good for man to be alone. I will make a helper suitable for him" Now the Lord God had formed out of the ground all the beasts of the field and all the birds of the air. He brought them to the man to see what he would name them; and whatever the man called each living creature, that was its name. So, the man gave names to all the livestock, the birds of the air, and all the beasts of the field. But for Adam, no suitable helper was found. So, the Lord God caused the man to fall into a deep sleep; and while he was sleeping, he took one of the man's ribs and closed up the place with flesh. Then the Lord God made a woman from the rib he had taken out of the man, and he brought her to the man."

Why is this important? Notice the order of events that happened in Genesis. God creates Adam, God places Adam in the Garden of Eden, God commands Adam not to eat of the tree of knowledge of good and evil, Adam names a bunch of animals and gets sad he doesn't have a partner, so God creates Eve. God instructed Adam on what he should not do and then created Eve. This means that Eve didn't hear God's instruction and needed Adam to teach her.

As we know from reading Genesis, Eve was later deceived by the serpent to disobey God and eat of the tree. But why was she so easily deceived? Because she was uneducated from lack of firsthand experience. Obviously, Adam didn't teach her (or didn't do a very good job) about the command from the Lord, because she was deceived by the serpent with a simple, "Did God really say…" question. She couldn't answer because she wasn't there. The lack of education within Eve led her to be easily deceived.

Bringing this back to Paul in the book of 1 Timothy. Why would Paul use Adam and Eve as an illustration? Paul earlier in the chapter outlines how he is an adequate teacher of the truth because of his experience and knowledge gained from Christ. In this era (62-64AD) women were uneducated. They were not allowed to attend seminary or higher education, nor were they allowed to hold any positions of esteem according to society.

Putting all these pieces together, it seems that Paul, when describing his ideal teacher of the word within Timothy's church, leans heavily on the importance of that person being educated, knowing the truth, and being of true faith. Women are a great example in this era of someone who is uneducated and would then be disqualified from teaching according to the standards outlined by Paul. He is telling Timothy that if someone is uneducated and lacks true faith, they should not teach.

Within our society today, women have the same access to education and are spiritually gifted in the same ways that men are. If Paul's main concern is the education of those who are teaching, using women as an example of those who would be uneducated would not hold up today.

There is one more component within this passage that is worth exploring, which is Paul's instruction for women to learn in silence. This can be explained within the context of the period in which it was written. When couples would attend temple gatherings, they would not sit together. Instead, men would sit with men and women would sit with women. Because women were uneducated and sitting in temples, they obviously would have questions to ask their husbands. Instead of women calling out across the room to ask their husbands questions, Paul is asking women to sit and learn in silence and ask questions after. This is a continuation of Paul's emphasis in many places throughout his letters which necessitates an "orderly" service that presents ample opportunity to sit in the presence of the Lord (1 Corinthians 14:26-40).

Women again are being used as an example by Paul to describe something that he needed to address. In this case, it was an example of how the church had been disorderly because of the number of people talking at the same time. This is more of a description of the gatherings at the time than a prescriptive measure meant to be applied to all church gatherings in the future. Noting how other women like Priscilla and Phoebe were carrying out their ministries by obviously using words, we can make the logical conclusion that he is not saying that women should be silent in the church in all circumstances.

Ephesians 5:

When Ephesians 5 gets brought up in conversation as it relates to women and their expected role in the Kingdom of God, most people start at 22 and stop at verse 24. However, reading the verse directly before and the verses after gives further context to the point that Paul is making in his letter to the Church in Ephesus.

Before, in verse 21:

"Submit to ***one another*** out of reverence for Christ."

After verse 24 (v.25-33):

"Husbands, love your wives, just as Christ loved the church and gave himself up for her to make her holy, cleansing her by the washing with water through the word, and to present her to himself as a radiant church, without stain or wrinkle or any other blemish, but holy and blameless. In this same way, husbands ought to love their lives as their own bodies. He who loves his wife loves himself. After all, no one ever hated his own body, but he feeds and cares for it, just as Christ does the church, for we are members of his body. "For this reason, a man will leave his father and mother and be united to his wife, and the two will become one flesh." This is a profound mystery but I am talking about Christ and the church. However, each one of you also must love his wife as he loves himself, and the wife must respect her husband."

Some use the passage in Ephesians to describe how a man's life and purpose are greater than a woman's. By emphasizing that it is simply a woman's role to submit to her husband, it would imply that a woman's value is somehow less than a man's. Ephesians 5:21-33 seemingly paints the opposite point.

From verse 21, Paul indicates that a healthy relationship between a husband and his wife is one of mutual submission. And that by doing so, they are glorifying Christ. The dynamic within Ephesians 5 shows us that the ideal dichotomy in a marriage is one where a husband puts his wife before himself and loves her the same way that he loves himself and then the wife submits to her husband. If you asked any wife in the world, if their husband was constantly seeking what was best for her, loving her well, treating her with the same respect, honor, and dignity that they do themselves, and caring for her with the attention to detail they care for themselves if they would have any problem submitting to that man, you would get a resounding "no." Where the dynamic breaks down in this paradigm is if either the man or the woman is waiting for the other to start following Paul's instructions first and won't hold up their end of the deal until the other does.

The ideal relationship that Paul is outlining requires a lot of trust because it depends on reciprocity. For it to function, the husband must sacrificially love his wife and the woman must sacrificially submit to her husband. But if both are steadfastly dedicated to upholding their end of the deal and following Christ first, they will have a healthy marriage that is centered around Christ.

How does this relate to a woman's role within leadership? If men and women are called to mutually submit to one another within the context of marriage, that means neither is greater or less than within that relationship. Men and women are equal in value within the dynamic that Paul outlines. By setting it up the way that he does, he emphasizes that each has a unique value and role within the relationship, but that both roles are worthy of equal mutual submission.

1 Corinthians 11:11-12

Within 1 Corinthians 11, Paul boils down the conversation about head coverings in a worship gathering. In doing so, in verses 11-12, Paul illuminates the fact that though women came from men, men are also born of women, and that in the end, everyone comes from God.

Following chapter 11, Paul discusses the use of spiritual gifts in chapter 12 and lists them out and their need for each other. There is no differentiation of gifts endowed to women or men based on gender but instead are given gifts that uniquely equip specific believers with gifts that they will use to love their neighbor, speak the truth in love, and lead others to the Gospel.

Whether it is women witnessing the resurrected Christ and sharing the Good News for the first time, Deborah leading the Israelites as a prophetess and judge, Phoebe going on missions to serve the Church, Esther courageously saving her people, Priscilla leading a house church, Naomi mentoring Ruth, Rahab boldly enabling the conquest of Canaan or Ruth emulating the heart of God, we see women littered throughout Scripture who hold the highest positions of prominence and making significant contributions to the Kingdom of God. In each instance, God either appointed them or put them in positions where only they could be the ones to carry out the calling on their lives at that specific time. After breaking down the verses that may seem to contradict that sentiment by analyzing the culture of the time and what seems to be Paul's main point within his writings, we can see that God's character and view towards women are the same throughout Scripture and Paul's words don't contradict that.

So how does Scripture inform our current culture's views on women in leadership? From analyzing passages from the Old and the New Testament it is clear that God does not hesitate to empower women in a myriad of situations and contexts where they are called to use their spiritual gifts to glorify God. From operating with authority in leadership, to how they strengthen the body and act with great courage in the face of adversity, God values women the same way that He values men.

In our society, even though there has been great progress toward women being seen equally to men, there are still those in our pews who are single, divorced, widowed, or even unattractive that are deemed "second class citizens" and treated differently because they do not fit into the mold of an "acceptable" woman within the church. Women with many strengths, gifts, talents, and passions are often placed on the sideline because of superficial reasons.

The reality is that the Church has much to learn from these women from all walks of life. The fortitude of a single mother, the strength of the widow, the perseverance of the unattractive. Women are judged severely by their outward appearance and any non-conformity to the norms of society will see them disqualified even within churches. The Bible makes clear that a woman's worth is not in her beauty or her willingness to conform to what society says she must be. But examples like Esther show us that the Lord cares far more about the character, integrity, and love of Him than any of those material standards.

Women are not relegated to just serving men in their existence. Their value and worth are not dictated by the approval or appointment of men. They are created in the image of God, fully empowered and strengthened to do exactly what God placed them on this planet to do. Reading through all the examples listed in Scripture, we see women teaching, preaching, leading, empowering, encouraging, creating, correcting, guiding, strengthening, and carrying out the will of God in their lives.

One cannot acknowledge some parts of Paul's teachings and not others. They can't disconnect the actions he took from the words he spoke. We must try to make sense of them both in the same context. It is easy to take verses from 1st Timothy or Ephesians out of context as a way of controlling a woman, but the reality is that Paul himself empowered women in his movement to be integral leaders within it. To rectify both truths together, there must be a further explanation. This in context shows that the verses seemingly telling women to be quiet and get out of the way are just examples of the time of people who were uneducated, easily deceived, and wanting to learn.

Classifying women as useless or only to be used by men to further themselves is not only wrong but also sinful. They have been created with the same intentionality, care, and empowerment that the Lord uses to breathe life into men. Women are valuable members of the body of Christ and have innumerable amounts of ways they are called to pour into their communities and churches should not get in the way of that. The Lord didn't.

Chapter 8

Eldership and Shared Governance

Brick:

Who is charged with leading the body of Christ? When elders are selected to be overseers in a congregation, what does the Bible say the selection committee should be looking for in their character, lives, and stature? What is the role of an elder? Is it intended that there only be one leader in charge of a congregation? What accountability structures should be in place for those in elder-type roles and other leadership within the church? Does church leadership represent their community?

Reason for analysis:

What the church elevates, it also supports and endorses. If elders and board seats are filled with people who don't match what Scripture says about who should fill them and what traits they should embody, those effects are felt through every aspect of how a church operates. If business acumen and worldly success are used as determining factors in the selection process over holiness and Christlikeness, the result will be a body that uses worldly success as a measure of their righteousness, which is wildly misguided. Even if an elder or pastor is selected using biblical principles, ministry "burnout" is still ravaging communities, leaving congregants feeling lost and confused when enough is enough and that leader leaves, oftentimes suddenly. There isn't enough support for those in leadership, which can also be seen in the accountability of said leaders. When only one or two voices can hold a leader accountable, or worse no accountability at all, abuse of many kinds will often follow. Paying attention to the news for an extended period, it is obvious that the church is seeing a crisis of leadership across the board. This leadership stagnation and failure can stem back to a myriad of reasons, but how leadership is selected, what accountability is in place for those leaders, and what example they lead with are core starting points to that conversation. Who is charged with the shepherding and guidance of the body of Christ is of utmost importance.

There are many conversations around "who" is allowed to be an elder. Debate continues constantly about whether only men can be elders, where women fit in, the difference between elders, pastors, and deacons, and depending on what denomination you claim, your "side" of those debates is going to differ. While that conversation has merit, and there is value in having that discussion, there are more pressing underlying issues to discuss when it comes to eldership. Primarily speaking, the Church in the United States is facing a crisis of leadership. Scandals and moral failures are plaguing churches, and congregations are left wondering why it happened and how it got to that point. This type of crisis doesn't just happen overnight and many things could have been put in place to avoid them. However, the process in which these leaders are elevated, to begin with, and how leadership teams are structured opens the door for these problems to arise. The role of an elder has looked less like a shepherd and more like a board that is more fit for a business.

Though there are financial aspects to running a church that are incredibly important, the focus of the body of Christ is not, has not, and should not be financial in any shape or form. There is certain diligence and wisdom that should be used when distributing funds, but the primary goal of an elder board is to shepherd their flock, not build up the bottom line. Being an elder is not like being on a board as a shareholder within a business. It should be someone who is in the trenches with a pulse of the congregation. The focus for an elder should be on empowering the body, praying for their congregation, overseeing ministries, serving the church, and bringing wisdom and discernment into decisions being made. But all too often, positions of leadership within churches are given to people who do not have the credentials listed in Scripture.

When selecting an elder, churches should be using the Scriptures to guide their choices. This is one of the rare cases where the New Testament writers are very prescriptive in their instructions for how to do something and churches should heed those words seriously. Determining who should be an elder, what their life should look like, and what characteristics they should embody are specifically broken down by multiple authors and in many different places throughout the letters of the New Testament.

In Titus 1, Paul outlines in verses 6-9, *"An elder must be blameless, the husband of but one wife, a man whose children believe and are not open to the charge of being wild and disobedient. Since an overseer is entrusted with God's work, he must be blameless-not overbearing, not quick-tempered, not given to drunkenness, not violent, not pursuing dishonest gain. Rather he must be hospitable, one who loves what is good, who is self-controlled, upright, holy and disciplined. He must hold firmly to the trustworthy message as it has been taught, so that he can encourage others by sound doctrine and refute those who oppose it."* He begins with an extremely high bar, and one would assume that is intentional. Being an elder is not for just anyone, and anybody that holds that position should not take that charge lightly. Reading through that list weeds out a large number of people and more than likely most of your congregants, which is the point. Those that churches put in places of leadership are called to a higher standard of living (James 3:1) and if there is nobody in your church that fits this bill, have fewer elders instead of forcing a square peg into a round hole of elevating someone that doesn't meet this criterion.

Paul adds further clarity to the mindset in even wanting to be an overseer of the church and outlines more specific criteria that selection committees should be looking for in 1 Timothy 3:1-7, *"Here is a trustworthy saying: If anyone sets his heart on being an overseer, he desires a noble task. Now that overseer must be above reproach, the husband of but one wife, temperate, self-controlled, respectable, hospitable, able to teach, not given to drunkenness, not violent but gentle, not quarrelsome, not a lover of money. He must manage his own family well and see that his children obey him with proper respect. (If anyone does not know how to manage his own family, how can he take care of God's church?) He must not be a recent convert, or he may become conceited and fall under the same judgment as the devil. He must also have a good reputation with outsiders, so that he will not fall into disgrace and into the devil's trap."* Within this expansion of Paul's criteria for elders of a church, there are some additions from his writings to Titus. For instance, Paul brings up that not only should the elder have strong character in a multitude of ways, but that the elder should have a respectable home and not be a recent convert. There is wisdom within these passages that anyone who has been in ministry for any length of time understands why those precautions are added to the list. When churches are selecting an elder, following a strict list of binary checkboxes won't bring the full picture of what should be looked for. There is an element of discernment and wisdom that should be brought to these selection committees from those who have been in the church for a long time, that have seen these things play out, and lend credence to their validity.

In Acts 14:23 we get to read a firsthand account of Paul and Barnabas appointing elders in Lystra, Iconium, and Antioch. It says, *"Paul and Barnabas appointed elders for them in each church and, with prayer and fasting, committed them to the Lord, in whom they put their trust."* In each city, Paul and Barnabas prayed and fasted as they appointed the elders of each of these cities. Throughout Scripture, when someone is fasting before or while they are doing something they were instructed by the Lord to do, that implies a level of conviction and seriousness that must be taken. Seeing this example clarifies the gravity of making these types of appointments within a congregation.

All the instructions that have been discussed thus far have been cut and dry. They feel like a bar to reach and objectively one can determine if a candidate has met them. But as with all things with the Lord, it is rarely ever just about our outward projections of ourselves. The Lord cares far more about the status of our hearts and the motives to which we do things than the physical tasks we carry out. Peter gets to this when appointing elders in 1 Peter 5:1-4 when he says, *"To the elders among you, I appeal as a fellow elder, a witness of Christ's sufferings and one who also will share in the glory to be revealed: Be shepherds of God's flock that is under your care, serving as overseers-not because you must, but because you are willing, as God wants you to be; not greedy for money, but eager to serve; not lording it over those entrusted to you, but being examples to the flock. And when the Chief Shepherd appears, you will receive the crown of glory that will never fade away."* When Peter begins his comments about eldership it is interesting to note that he starts by appealing to his "fellow" elders insinuating that he too is an elder. He skips over the checklist of traits they are called to live by and instead addresses their hearts. Probably from experience, Peter emphasizes that being an overseer or an elder should be something that you want to do, not have to do. Those who fill these positions are aptly placed in a position that must be sensitive to the body and the needs that arise and doing so from a heart of "having to" will only create problems in the future. He then addresses the obvious power dynamic that is all too easy to rear its ugly head by charging elders with a focus on service and not "lording it over" those they serve. Putting into perspective that these people have been entrusted into an elder's care and their example is of utmost importance. The heart behind leading in such a fashion is just as important as living the life of righteousness that Paul deliberately breaks down.

What does that service look like? James and Paul both outline specific tasks that elders are responsible for. In James 5:14 he says, *"Is any one of you sick? He should call the elders of the church to pray over him and anoint him with oil in the name of the Lord"* and Paul in 1 Timothy 4:14 says, *"Do not neglect your gift, which was given you through a prophetic message when the body of elders laid their hands on you."* This is obviously not an exhaustive list of all of what elders are responsible for, but it does give the reader a glimpse into some of the roles that they play within the body. James shows us that elders are called to pray for the sick and needy and anoint people with oil on behalf of the Lord. Paul takes it a step further by describing what happened to Timothy, which was elders laying their hands on him and empowering him to use the gift given to him by the Lord. There may not be a complete list of all the tasks an elder may complete, but from these passages and others that discuss the role of shepherds, we can glean not only the type of person for this type of role but also how they are supposed to carry it out.

An elder is supposed to be an overseer and a servant. One who brings wisdom and discernment into the decision-making and direction of the Church. Who empowers the body to use their spiritual gifts and pray for those they shepherd. They should have the fruit of someone who is constantly striving to be more like Christ, laying down their life and serving others. Where their Christlikeness is more important than any worldly credentials or success. Obviously, is not perfect but has the humility to take ownership of mistakes, repent, ask for forgiveness, and reconcile situations where they have been wrong. This is a tall order!

Oftentimes when leaders and elders are being selected, worldly success and acumen are attractive to these selection committees. A common trend churches have seen recently is an influx of business owners, entrepreneurs, and largely successful (and wealthy) people in a worldly sense rising in leadership within their congregations. Being successful in business is not disqualifying, nor is it a bad thing in and of itself, but if boards and elders are filled with people whose focus is business, it is no surprise that churches end up looking like businesses themselves. Elders should represent the community that they lead, with diverse backgrounds of age, race, and occupations. Having a multitude of life experiences, vantage points and worldviews will help not just in the decision-making, but also in the eldership's ability to relate and minister to all demographics within their church.

Having discussed all the necessary credentials and heart space for becoming an elder, the practical implementation of bringing them on has proven to be of extreme importance. When constructing an elder board and writing the necessary bylaws that accompany that work, strategy and safeguards are going to be the firm foundation the team can lean on in times of turbulence. It is not a matter of if your church will go through leadership hardship, it is when. And if bi-laws and structure are put in place beforehand, it makes going through those seasons a lot easier.

There are legal requirements for setting up a church and its leadership, like a 501(c)(3) and bylaws, but generally, most churches also have statements of faith, outlines of their doctrine and theology, and overall construction of the church. How things have been constructed and carried out is similar in most denominations, but Scripture doesn't outline those items specifically. For example, the Bible doesn't list out how many elders a church should have or even who oversees elevating them. It doesn't specifically say that a church should be led by just one person or if there is room for many. The Bible doesn't outline these things because there is no one "right way" to construct a church. Following the Lord gives us three sets of foundational truths for us to follow: The core of orthodoxy (primary theology), prescriptive commands, and examples for us to imitate (or not). Everything else is secondary doctrine and things that we can disagree on, but still call each other brothers and sisters in Christ, and the appointment of eldership is one of them.

If we all hold to the prescriptive qualities outlined in the New Testament for the type of leader we elevate, the rest falls into the preference category. There are many dynamics that lead to making these decisions, but we find ourselves in a state of urgency with countless examples of abuse coming out almost weekly. Maybe it is time to re-evaluate how these preferences are being carried out. One of which is, how many people are involved in leadership?

For most churches, there are different layers of leadership, whether that be deaconship, eldership, service teams, worship leaders, pastors, etc. that all have varying degrees of power and influence. But in most instances, there is one singular pastor at the top. This monarchical leadership structure has many positives, like decisions being easily made, only having one vision to follow, etc. but it has also led to devastating loss and abuse. A shared governance approach has problems of its own but also has credibility as a method to run a church.

In this scenario, the power and influence are shared among a small group of people, again exact numbers are not specifically given for a reason, everybody is going to be different. But with more people involved, there is increased accountability among that small group of leaders. This also would help by sharing the responsibility load. Even the pastors and elders that are doing it right are "burning out" at an alarming rate. Some godly men and women are leaving the ministry in droves because of how exhausted they've been running the church. This alleviates the "celebrity" culture temptation that has been so pervasive in the United States that elevates a personality and a brand over the truth and elevation of Jesus. If the church is led by a group of elders, it would be much harder for any one person to be elevated more than they should. This also opens the door to bi-vocational ministry, where pastors and elders can share responsibilities, but also work other jobs outside of the church. The more leaders that are elevated in this way, the more leeway it gives leaders to work and provide a living without needing to take a salary from the church. What if there were no salaries paid by tithe money at all and all money that was taken in the basket was used for benevolence, church function, and administrative needs? It is interesting to note that in 1 Timothy 5:17 when Paul says, *"The elders who direct the affairs of the church well are worthy of double honor, especially those whose work is preaching and teaching."* he notates elder(s) not elder singular when discussing the work of teaching and preaching. And that when Jesus sent out his disciples, he sent them off in pairs and not by themselves.

Again, it isn't wrong to have a church that has a singular leader that is supported by other leaders in multiple roles, but there may be other ways to approach constructing a leadership team that may give more life to the Church and the leaders who run it. The Bible is not clear that it should be run one way or the other from either Testament. One could point to God's usage of Kings in the Old Testament but remember that God was reluctant to appoint those Kings because He desired to be their King and their King alone, but the Israelites wanted a man to lead them. And on the other side of that coin, it can be pointed out that before Kings were appointed over Israel, God ordained Judges to help lead his people, which in most cases existed at the same time as one another. There can be arguments on both sides because both sides have validity and at the end of the day, churches should be constructed by how the Bible outlines they should and what the conviction of the Holy Spirit says for the rest. But regardless of how the governance ends up being constructed, the elevation of elders is abundantly clear for how churches should proceed.

Elders should have the pulse of their congregation. They should know what struggles exist, what problems have arisen, who needs support, and who needs to be empowered. When people in the body are in crisis, elders should be first with prayer and support and in the trenches with them, not because they must, but because they have a genuine desire to serve the body. The elders should represent their community, varying in age, race, and occupation to achieve a diverse outlook that serves all demographics in their body. Bringing wisdom and discernment into decision making, being willing to toil over following the Lord's teachings and guidance in everything the church does. And last, but not least, they should be striving to be Christ-like in all they do and have the fruit of a seasoned believer to follow the Lord with everything they have.

The Church is in desperate need of people who fit the criteria laid out in Scripture to step up and serve the local church they are a part of. Only a few will meet that criterion, but those people are such a gift to the bodies that they serve. There is no greater work than to love those God has called elders to love and to serve them in a way that is glorifying to Him.

Chapter 9

Abuse

Brick:

Why is there abuse running rampant through congregations of all different kinds of denominations? Why does it seem like we are hearing about abuse happening in the church with greater frequency? How does the Church deal with abuse? How does the Bible address issues of abuse? As believers, what is our role in dealing with issues of abuse?

Reason for analysis:

In the 21st century, the accessibility to information and the ability to share one's story with the world within minutes has exposed an underlying current of abuse throughout the Church. There is little doubt that it has been there all along, but because people can share their stories and find others with similar stories within a short time, more and more people are describing horrific instances of abuse within their time in the church. Three massive problems revolve around the issue of abuse within the Church in America:

1. First and foremost, the biggest issue is that abuse happens at all within the Church.
2. That when abuse happens, the Church is often more worried about the ramifications and fall out of the exposure of the abuse than the abuse itself.
3. The current system for how the Church is run in the United States is set up in a way that allows abuse to happen and for it to be covered up easily.

Before breaking down the many different facets of abuse with the Church, it is important to define terms. The Oxford Dictionary defines abuse as "treating a person with cruelty or violence, especially regularly or repeatedly." It is important to define what abuse is because if we call any negative experience we have "abuse," that changes the gravity of the word. So, in the case of the Church, when discussing abuse, it breaks down into three main types: sexual, emotional (or verbal), and spiritual. In each case of what we define as "abuse," the abuser must have power or authority over that person, whether by title, age, or a personal sense of superiority over the abused.

Sexual abuse within the Church is rightly scandalous. These are the stories that grab headlines and draw the ire of attention for a few days and then society quickly moves on. In the 21st century, it feels like one of these stories drops right after the last one cools off. The reason why these stories are scandalous is that there are criminal ramifications, and this type of abuse is denounced across the spectrum by everyone regardless of their background or religious affiliations. Most people can agree that sexual abuse of any kind is wrong and should have hefty consequences. These instances are not rare, and statistics show us that we only know about a small percentage of the events that are happening. In a report that outlines protestant church insurers handling upwards of 260 sexual abuse cases a year that cover over 224,000 churches in the United States, the author describes the under-reporting phenomena. "Even with hundreds of cases a year "that's a very small number. That probably doesn't even constitute half," said Gary Schoener, director of the Walk-In Counseling Center in Minneapolis, a consultant on hundreds of Protestant and Catholic clergy misconduct cases. "Sex abuse in any domain, including the church, is reported seldom. We know a small amount actually came forward."

The shame that comes with coming forward with a story of sexual abuse is what typically holds someone back from doing so. In most cases, manipulation occurs where the abuser convinces the abused that if they were to come forward, "A productive ministry would be destroyed" or "all the people they could help, can no longer be helped if they are removed from their position" or "God's plan will be hindered in their lives" or any other number of reasons or rationales given to excuse the abuse. This form of manipulation multiplies and keeps leaders in power for much longer than they should.

Outside of the abuse itself, the most disappointing aspect of situations like this is that oftentimes the abused believe that all they need to do is come forward and shine a light on the issue and it will be resolved or be taken care of. But what we've seen as a society, is that in most cases it takes many more victims and far more publicity for those who have abused others to see any change take place. When boards and elders are made aware of these situations, they have a choice to make, and they normally fall into four different categories:

1. Believe the victim(s), place the leader on administrative leave, investigate, and take necessary actions.
2. Believe the victim(s), justify the actions of the abuser, defend the accused, and do what is necessary to make the issue go away.
3. Don't believe the victim(s), continue business as normal, push the victim(s) out of any role of influence within the church, separate that person from any ministry they are involved in, and act like it never happened.

4. Don't believe the victim(s) and pretend the issue never even came up.

The main reason why this brick needs to be analyzed is that in far too many cases, leadership teams follow options 2-4, far more than option 1. There is a business concept that when related to the economy carries over into this conversation. This is the concept of being "too big to fail." In economical scenarios, this is when a business has too large of influence in the entirety of the economy, where if they failed individually, that would create a domino effect that would destroy the entire system. At this point, the government will take that failure upon themselves and figure out a way to "bail out" that company so that they won't fail. This logic has been used time and time again for pastors who run large ministries and has led to substantial fallout.

Within churches around the country, some believe that their pastor or leader is "too big to fail." Where they convince themselves that if they were to remove that leader from their position it would cause a domino effect that would lead to the whole ministry failing. If that is true about an organization, the truth is, they probably would be better off failing. Ministry is not supposed to revolve around any one person other than Jesus. Period. If a ministry is built in such a way, that if one person fails and is removed, the entire entity would fail, that ministry wasn't built in the right way, to begin with. As Christ's followers, Jesus is always our head, and we are His body. No matter how we construct the leadership below Him, the fact remains, that Jesus must be our ultimate source of leadership.

When predatory leaders feel like they are untouchable, that is typically when abuse that has been swept under the rug escalates and gets worse. It is sin and it acts like such. When Christians fall into sin, it is typically not the worst thing first. We see this with people that struggle with addictions. It always starts as something menial, and it develops into something larger and more destructive as time goes on. The "high" is not enough on its own, and it always requires the next

115

escalation to achieve that same high over time. Leaders that get away with abuse tend to have far more victims in their wake that were abused in much smaller ways that led to the instances that we see in the news. It is the lack of accountability that the Church has for its leaders that leads to situations where predators can leverage their power to abuse the susceptible.

Being in a position that deals with people in their mess, their most vulnerable moments, pastors, and leaders in a church are in a unique position that wields a lot of power. This power is to influence, guide, instruct, and walk alongside congregants through literally the best and worst times in their lives. With this kind of power, choices are made that can change the trajectory of someone's path that may never be altered. When lay people invite their pastors and leaders into their varying situations, they are unknowingly handing the keys over to their souls. This is not to be taken lightly. The pastors and leaders who recognize this power and use it to guide people back to Christ and the truth, do work that will be remembered in people's lives forever and is blessed Kingdom work. But it also opens the possibility of that power being used to abuse people when they are extremely vulnerable.

Those who get caught up in situations where they are being abused by leaders oftentimes can't see it while it is happening. Because it happens slowly and over time, most abusers "groom" those who they are abusing to normalize certain behaviors or conversations. These situations are difficult to break down and have an enormous amount of nuance. Most of the time, abusers help their victims find freedom or help them in some way that makes them feel like they owe something to them. This will cause them to stay, even when all signs point toward leaving. They stay because they have experienced life-altering transformation in some way and can point to many positive experiences with their abuser as a way of explaining away their inappropriate actions or words. Gaslighting, manipulative conversations, using guilt and shame, and convincing the victim that they are the problem are all ways that they get away with these actions for far longer than they should. But in retrospect, it is common to hear abuse survivors claim that they should have seen the warning signs all along.

Human nature and sin dictate that it is impossible to prevent all instances of abuse. Churches should go to any length possible to decrease the probability of these events from happening, but it will continue if broken, imperfect human beings are at the helm. With that being said, the Church should not take the stance of, "well, it's going to happen anyway, what can we do about it?" Even though it will continue to happen, how the Church goes about handling these conversations and instances needs a dramatic overhaul that will change the quantity of these traumatic encounters happening.

For too long, leaders have used the historical account of David and Saul to illustrate why "loyalty" and "honor" are prerequisites for being in ministry. 1 Samuel 24 gets used frequently and parallels are drawn between David choosing not to kill Saul because Saul was still the God-anointed King of Israel and David had not yet taken the throne. Some pastors demand the same kind of loyalty from their staff. Things are said about how David not only honored the position but also had a certain reverence for Saul as King that prevented him from striking him down when he had the chance. The difficulty in these conversations is that (like all manipulation) there is a kernel of truth to be found in those statements.

David did honor Saul in those moments. He did have profound respect for God's anointed and had no desire to interfere with another man's calling from God. Though David had the means to kill Saul, he never took it upon himself to speed up God's timeline for his reign. All those things are true about the historical account of David choosing not to kill Saul. But the application of that account to modern-day churches and pastors is wrong from not only an exegetical standpoint but also from a practical one.

First, pastors are not Kings. Yes, God places people in authority, we know this from Romans 13. But the difference between the positions of a shepherd and the King of a nation is vast. Secondly,

David did not make the choices he did because of any kind of loyalty to Saul himself, but rather to God. David knows that his allegiance is to God first and earthly kingdoms second. So, David not killing Saul had far more to do with his obedience to God than it did with any lingering feelings about Saul's reign. When pastors or church leaders use this account as an example of why a congregant or leader shouldn't challenge a lack of accountability, that shows that they are far more concerned about keeping their title and position than they are in righteousness. Loyalty to any one leader or pastor above the Lord is idolatry. Addressing issues of abuse and conducting matters in a way that is glorifying Christ, by seeking justice and truth, is not only suggested but also mandatory.

If the Church came down hard on leaders who abused their congregants on a large scale, the likelihood of abuse continuing to happen in those congregations would substantially decrease. The reason why this issue continues to plague churches in the United States is that for as long as churches have existed in this country, there has been abuse that gets swept under the rug and minimized. Where does this come from? Again, the amount of nuance in these situations makes it difficult to give wide-sweeping truths that are going to apply to all situations.

People come to church and hopefully, they encounter God in all kinds of ways. There can be miraculous healings, marriages that are saved from the brink of divorce, long-lost children returning to Christ, lifelong relationships built, memories made and a bond as strong as a family. When congregants experience this type of community and all that comes with it, it is only natural to want to defend that entity. Even if there is abuse that is going on that everyone knows is wrong and should be dealt with, oftentimes board members and those in leadership would rather make a decision that would save the entity that they've had so much transformation in than deal with the abuser in an appropriate way. When people ask why situations like this happen for as long as they do, it is because of this dynamic where people experience profound moments in the same place that these horrible instances of abuse are happening.

When the decision is made to protect the entity instead of protecting the abused and providing them justice, further harm is done to the victim. Not only have they been abused by someone entrusted to care for them, but now that entity that has brought them life, transformation, healing, etc. turns its back on them too. So where do they go? Most of the time, they go nowhere. The victims realize that nothing is going to happen, so they stop fighting. The courage and strength it takes just to come forward in the first place is often all they can muster, and so they stop. That is until there is one who doesn't stop. One who says that no matter what happens, they will get their story out. So, when addressing the abuse with the abuser and church leadership goes nowhere, they reach out to authorities and the media. They begin to tell their story to anyone that will listen. And when they do, many Christians will say, "Why can't they just keep this all in the house?" or "This just makes the church look bad, why would they bring this into the public eye?" and even worse "They are probably just making this up to get attention and bring down "fill in the blank" because "fill in the blank...."

Even though statistics show that only between 2-8% of accusations of abuse are false according to The National Sexual Violence Resource Center, when multiple people come forward about the same abuser, that number plummets to under 1%. So, the odds are, that if church leadership hears about abuse happening in the congregation by someone in their ranks, it probably is. And if multiple people are lodging similar complaints and accusations, it almost assuredly is. When that first bold victim comes forward with their story and others who experienced similar things hear it, that generally leads to them coming forward as well. These issues cannot be taken lightly, regardless of who is being accused.

If it became commonplace for leaders in the church to appropriately investigate instances of abuse when complaints are first lodged, the abuse would be less likely to happen. The environment of blind loyalty and honor towards a leader is toxic and leads to situations where abuse is far more likely to happen. But what do these instances of abuse look like? As listed above, the simplest categories to break them down into are physical or sexual abuse, emotional or verbal abuse, and spiritual abuse.

The abuse that we all see on tv and in movies and what is most common when this topic is brought up is physical or sexual abuse. This is the most binary version of abuse and is the easiest to identify. That by no means indicates that it is the easiest to deal with, nor the easiest to talk about. But when talking about issues of abuse, this version is the one that is universally accepted, and most people can agree on what it looks like. Physically intimidating or harming someone that you have power over, is abuse. When a position or relational power dynamic leads to a form of physical attack, that can be defined as physical abuse. This typically takes place in marriages or families, where ties are especially deep and there are no outside influences in the home. If church leadership is privy to information that could lead to a conclusion that one of its members is physically abusing someone, that not only has to be taken seriously, but it also needs to be taken to the authorities immediately. That type of accusation is not something that can be taken care of "in-house." The proper authorities need to be made aware of it and it needs to be handled with efficacy and with great care.

Sexual abuse has similar legal ramifications. Especially in cases where kids are involved or if the event is heinous, law enforcement needs to be involved in the resolution of the accusation. There are no exceptions to this. Even if accusations are brought forward that are proven to be false, the chance cannot be taken that it is true. If there really is no abuse happening, the evidence will yield that result. In reading that section, there may be a response that goes something like, "But that person's reputation will be ruined" or "The church will be marred by an allegation like that" and that kind of response could not be further from the truth. The church taking an allegation like that seriously does far more good for the congregation as a whole than sweeping it under the rug or keeping it in-house would ever do. First, it decreases the likelihood of abuse happening in the congregation. Second, it tells people that if something were to happen to them, the church would have their back. And lastly, it tells the congregation that justice, truth, and righteousness are of greater worth to the leadership team than reputation, title, and loyalty to any single person other than Christ. Though these conversations can be excruciating to have and for the right thing to be done, dealing with physical or sexual abuse needs to be taken care of with the utmost seriousness.

The next type of abuse is a lot more difficult to define and nail down. Verbal or emotional abuse is far more prevalent in not just our churches, but also in our society. It doesn't have the same legal ramifications and it is substantially more difficult to prove. When a leader uses their power and authority to minimize, belittle, mock, or publicly tear someone down it can take on many forms. Most of the time this type of behavior is guised as a joke or an attempt to be funny. It absolutely can be in a fit of rage or berating that verbal or emotional abuse can take place, but those who abuse people in this way are far more cunning in how they use their words. Whether it be through gaslighting which leads to people thinking being abused is somehow their fault or the manipulation of someone's emotions by playing to their fears or areas of weakness. Emotionally abusing people can lead to lifelong trauma. In an environment that is meant to emulate Christ and how He treated people, this type of abuse should not be taking place. However, the struggle with this type of abuse comes with nuance. Is all teasing or joking abusive? No, it isn't. But it happens far more often than we give it credit for. We allow things to go on until it reaches a breaking point for the person being abused in this way. If this type of abuse is happening among the ranks of church leadership or anyone with spiritual authority in the church, it needs to be addressed and dealt with.

This brings the last type of abuse to the forefront: spiritual. In the unique position that people who lead the church find themselves, oftentimes people will look to said leaders to be a conduit for their relationship with Christ. They will wait for them to usher them into times with the Lord, they will look for words of knowledge to come from those people instead of going to the Lord themselves, they will ask for prophecy and other moments for them to grasp onto. Being in church leadership generally means that there will be situations where congregants are looking for those leaders to lead them spiritually. Obviously, this cannot be taken lightly. Spiritual abuse happens when a leader decides to use this uniquely powerful position to influence a congregant to do what they want them to do by using their platform and spiritual authority. By saying things like, "The Lord told me that you are supposed to "fill in the blank" or "I'm supposed to "fill in the blank" because the Lord told me to" or "I had this word of knowledge given to me by the Lord about "fill in the blank," so now I need you to "fill in the blank." People in a congregation give more credence to their leaders than they are supposed to. Instead of seeing themselves as a part of the Royal Priesthood (1 Peter 2:9) and being able to access God the same way that their leaders can, they believe that their leaders have a connection to the Lord that isn't attainable for them. So, the next best thing is to have access to that leader. When using any statements of "The Lord told me to tell you…" one must be incredibly careful to speak the truth that aligns with Scripture, doesn't benefit them in any way, and be with pinpoint accuracy. If you have a word for someone that doesn't fit that criterion, continue praying until you do. It is dangerous and blasphemous to talk on behalf of the Lord when He is not the one influencing you to do so. Spiritually manipulating people can lead to severe mistrust with not only the Church but with God Himself because the abused may assign their disappointment with words that never came to fruition onto God, even though it came from a false place.

Whether the abuse is physical, sexual, verbal, emotional, or spiritual, it all needs to be taken seriously by those in church leadership. The Church is meant to be a place where all people, from all walks of life, feel safe to worship and fellowship with other believers, knowing that if a situation were to arise, those in leadership would handle it appropriately. First and foremost, the appropriate way starts with believing the abused first, investigating second, and executing proper discipline when needed. But the other important aspect of abuse is attempting to prevent it in the first place. The reason why abuse has run rampant in congregations, to begin with, is because of a lack of accountability amongst church leaders.

Abuse in the church is a systemic issue. If the product of the current system in the United States continues to churn out case after case of abuse of all forms, that means there is a problem in the system. When churches are centered around the ego and ability of one leader and the church is seen more as a business than a place of worship and the reputation of the name comes first, abuse is going to run rampant. And it is because when a church is operating in that fashion, those who care about upholding the entity will do whatever is necessary to protect it. This means that any cases of abuse need to be handled in-house, authorities are not brought in, events are minimized and discounted into non-existence and victims are hushed into thinking they are alone, and nobody will believe them. This system must be overhauled with integrity, character, and most of all hearts seeking to glorify Christ. If abuse continues to run unchecked in our congregations, the Church will continue to be marred in the public square. It will not be taken seriously, and people will not feel like the Church is a safe place.

Regardless if we are in leadership or not, all Christians should seek to end abuse in all forms. Whether that is in our own lives, our own families, or within the walls of our churches. In no way, can any type of abuse co-exist with a relationship with Christ. It is sinful and it is idolatrous to choose loyalty to man rather than to God and justice. The Church is meant to be a safe haven for all who come, the broken, the dirty and unclean, the vulnerable, and the abused. It is the responsibility of those who are in church leadership to facilitate an environment where those people can encounter Christ for themselves and find healing from the abuse they have encountered, not endure more.

Chapter 10

Bivocational Ministry and Resources

Brick:

Was being a pastor ever meant to be a full-time vocation? How were the disciples/church planters/missionaries compensated compared to now? Is the Church in the United States using its resources for Gospel-centric work? How many people are using their spiritual gifts within the body when putting on a normal Sunday morning? What is tithe money intended for?

Reason for Analysis:

Finance meetings at churches are probably one of the least attended gatherings of churches today. But it is within those meetings that congregants can see how their church is using the resources given to them and hopefully bring accountability where there needs to be. The allocation of large sums of money within a church context is a sensitive topic and for most, they'd rather just not engage at all. But in the era of celebrity pastors and mega churches, tens of millions of dollars can be in motion within these ministries. A church doesn't need to be a mega-church or have millions of dollars to work with to have issues with the deployment of church resources. Quick queries of pastors' salaries within mega churches reveal that some are making between $250-$650k a year and that is without book deals, seminars, and conferences built-in. Exorbitant salaries are only one aspect of how churches can be mishandling finances. Some would argue that the scale of the size of the church justifies the salaries being given out, but that would only be true if the church were a business, which it is not. Within these financial dynamics, it is typically the "face" of the church that is making the most audacious of salaries, but it doesn't end there. Even if a specific church isn't handing out six-digit salaries, there is still the issue of pastors having the temptation to dilute truth in their sermons because they know that if they were to preach exactly what they were called to, the biggest givers in the church may leave. And because their livelihood and family's well-being are dependent on that salary, a rational person can't blame them for contemplating that temptation and giving in to it. If the majority of church resources are being used on salaries, that oftentimes leaves little resources for the actual ministries within the church, which leads churches to raise additional funds from special tithes and donations. The financial burdens that the Church experiences both in plenty and in want are very real and have very tangible consequences. How churches are utilizing their finances may not be in line with what New Testament authors outlined in their writings to the leaders of that day. Yet those principles still hold, and churches may find it best to analyze how they operate and seek where potential changes need to be made.

The current paradigm of most churches in the United States is for the church to have a few full-time staff members (the more attended church is, the more full-time staff) and those individuals are responsible for running the church. There is typically one leader that gives direction to the church, calls the shots and everyone else works off that vision. More times than not there are positions in youth ministry, women's and men's ministry, children's ministry, administration, worship ministry, young adult's ministry, outreach, and more. Obviously, there is plenty of work to be done and needs to be met in each of those categories of ministry. And the church in the US has largely solved that problem in similar ways that the world would solve them. Employment. But what does Scripture say about how we solve this problem?

When discussing this issue, most people bring up the same five sections of Scripture from the New Testament. They are used to justify why pastors are being paid at all, however the importance of bringing this topic up is not whether pastors should be paid, but the methods by which they are paid and to what extent.

1 Corinthians 9:9-14

"For it is written in the Law of Moses, "You shall not muzzle an ox when it treads out the grain." Is it for oxen that God is concerned? 10 Does he not certainly speak for our sake? It was written for our sake because the plowman should plow in hope and the thresher threshes in hope of sharing in the crop. 11 If we have sown spiritual things among you, is it too much if we reap material things from you? 12 If others share this rightful claim on you, do not we even more? Nevertheless, we have not made use of this right, but we endure anything rather than put an obstacle in the way of the gospel of Christ.13 Do you not know that those who are employed in the temple service get their food from the temple and those who serve at the altar share in the sacrificial offerings? 14 In the same way, the Lord commanded that those who proclaim the gospel should get their living by the gospel."

Luke 10:7

"And remain in the same house, eating and drinking what they provide, for the laborer deserves his wages. Do not go from house to house."

2 Thessalonians 3:7-10

"For you yourselves know how you ought to imitate us, because we were not idle when we were with you, 8 nor did we eat anyone's bread without paying for it, but with toil and labor we worked night and day, that we might not be a burden to any of you. 9 It was not because we do not have that right, but to give you in ourselves an example to imitate.10 For even when we were with you, we would give you this command: If anyone is not willing to work, let him not eat."

Acts 6:2

"And the twelve summoned the full number of the disciples and said, "It is not right that we should give up preaching the word of God to serve tables."

Philippians 4:16-19

"Even in Thessalonica you sent me help for my needs once and again.17 Not that I seek the gift, but I seek the fruit that increases to your credit. 18 I have received full payment, and more. I am well supplied, having received from Epaphroditus the gifts you sent, a fragrant offering, a sacrifice acceptable and pleasing to God. 19 And my God will supply every need of yours according to his riches in glory in Christ Jesus."

Though it may not be "wrong" or "sinful" to pay full-time wages to those in ministry, one must consider whether it is "wise." When a substantial amount of tithe money coming in, is dedicated to paying salaries and separate offerings are needed to give benevolence, the balance of things may be out of whack. Our society has made being a pastor more of a vocation than a calling. Book deals, guest appearances, exorbitant six-digit salaries, and expensive clothing make being a pastor something to be desired for worldly reasons. When being a pastor should be a calling on one's life that comes with the sacrifice of the ways of this world being first and foremost.

The disciples lived as full-time missionaries and as shown in the verses above, they weren't looking to make missionary work a profitable venture, but just their normal needs met. We don't know the background of all the disciples, but we do know that they came from all lines of work. When they originally followed Jesus, some of them never stopped working those jobs. There were some like Matthew who left his post as a tax collector to follow Christ without returning, but we know that Peter, James, and John (among others) were fishermen and from time to time did return to fishing.

Paul is the best example when looking for an alternative method of running a ministry within the New Testament. He had a past of being a Pharisee within the ranks of Judaism when he first interacted with Jesus, but he was also known as a tent maker. While he was moving from town to town preaching the gospel, he did everything he could to not be a burden on the towns he was serving (2 Thessalonians 3:8) and used his occupation of tent-making to offset the costs needed for him to live (Acts 18:1-3; 20:33-35; Philippians 4:14-16). Money was never an obstacle for Paul's ministry both in cost and profit. He was able to move freely, working and making a living (in the true essence of that word) and preaching the gospel.

When a pastor's salary and family's livelihood are tied to tithe money, it is easy to give in to the temptation of tickling ears and not teaching the truth. Nobody would like to imagine that they'd give in to the pressures of leading people in a way that was correlated to their income, but it is extremely difficult to separate the two. Even if it is never acted upon, the temptation being present at all shows that when money is involved in the creation of sermons and teachings, there is way too much room for that to go awry. Wanting to protect the ability to provide for your family is innately present in how God created us as humans, but if our convictions can be influenced by the handful of people that represent most of the tithe each week, the fullness of the gospel is not being preached. The Gospel is offensive and if preached correctly should impact and convict all of us in ways that we all need. This means those who are the biggest givers should also be tested in their faith, convictions, ideology, theology, and worldview. But if there is even one of them who doesn't like being corrected in that way and makes that known, the temptation to cater to that individual can feel unbearable.

As shown by the passages above, it is biblical to compensate workers for their efforts and ministry is no exception. So how does the Church structure paying their workers, but not in an exorbitant way that mirrors how businesses compensate their highest-ranked employees? Ironically the decentralization of power as noted in the chapter on "Shared Governance" is a good place to start. If more workers are working fewer hours, spreading out appropriate pay, that shares the responsibilities of leading, which empowers more people in the body to live within their giftings and raises more disciplers who train and disciple more disciplers it can lessen the financial burden on the church while still completing the necessary work of ministry. Part of the dynamic at play that prevents this type of structure is the desire to have just one person and personality lead a church. But as we've seen time and time again, when a local church is led by one domineering personality that is overly compensated and the entire ministry revolves around, that more times than not leads to pride, ego, and unfortunately abuse in many forms. Even those who don't fall into the trap of personality, the one appointed to lead their community often experience burnout and isolation where they feel like they can't reach out, be truly vulnerable or express any type of hardship that may taint their leadership.

To think outside of the box, what would it look like to spend less on salaries, get more people involved utilizing their spiritual gifts/talents, spread the workload, share the stage, and function in bodies where 90% of the people do 10% of the work, instead of the 10% doing all the work for the 90%? The Church is not meant to be an entertainment source, like a play, where actors/actresses get on stage and perform for the audience. The Church is a living, breathing organism of people, all of which have strengths, gifts, and talents to offer the body, but oftentimes are not given the opportunity because all the work/influence has been consolidated into just a few positions. With the decentralization of power would come individuals who share the responsibility of leading while also working jobs outside of the church. This solves a multitude of issues that arise from having so many full-time workers on staff.

One thing bi-vocational ministry brings is the freedom of a staff member to pursue making a good living outside of the church, which has no bearing on what they make from the church. They'd be free to teach the hard truths, challenge the status quo and exercise their giftings without being worried about their living being impacted. Their family's well-being would never be in jeopardy from the standpoint of how they work in the church, which means their mentality would be more about them serving the church than the church serving them. It also allows for more people to pitch in and add to the body, utilizing their strengths where needed and allowing other people to lead where they are weak. In today's era, we expect pastors to be excellent shepherds, teachers, preachers, mentors, encouragers, and advocates, but the likelihood of a pastor having all those giftings and doing them well is almost zero to none. This means we are asking pastors to live and work outside of their giftings, which generally isn't a benefit to anyone. If a pastoral team could acknowledge the strengths and weaknesses of every elder a part of the team, and then delegated out responsibilities based on those findings, ideally, every ministry and aspect of the pastorate would be covered by someone that is gifted in that area. And where there is overlap, those elders would share the responsibility, so that serving the church in that way, on top of having a full-time job would not be too burdensome. For those that would claim that there isn't enough time, and it would be too big of a burden, it would illuminate to whom it is a calling and to whom it is an occupation. If it is your calling, it comes naturally, it is something that brings you joy and you relish the opportunity to use your giftings. But burn out being a major concern of church staff today, is more due to overwork and asking them to do things outside of their giftings than is the time dedicated towards it.

Another huge benefit, especially with scandal all around us, is that having an elder team that shares the load as bi-vocational pastors substantially increases accountability. Within current dynamics, even if someone on staff did witness abusive behavior in a head pastor and wanted to say something, the odds are that if they said something, they'd lose their job long before the pastor they are trying to hold accountable. When a church or system becomes too big, the leader becomes "too big to fail" and all kinds of allowances are given that would never be extended to someone much lower on the org chart of a ministry. If all elders on the pastoral team had equal power and the ability to hold each other accountable, where the ministry didn't just revolve around one personality being successful, abuse of all kinds would substantially diminish. Lastly, leading in such a way leads the church to constantly be looking to empower the congregation to use their giftings. If there is constant need and capacity, there will be constant fill. If a church is led by a pastoral team with equal power, equal stipends, and buy-in, it can focus more on what it was designed to do in the first place, and that is ministry.

For most churches, tithe money percentage-wise goes towards salaries and other staff expenditures. Which oftentimes leads to situations where there aren't as many resources to go towards ministry itself. What if the Church were to flip this dynamic on its head and spend most of its resources on ministry and the smallest percentage go towards stipends for the time those on staff are spending on doing the work? The current state of resource distribution within churches is built on four pillars: salaries, buildings, decoration, and equipment. All those components revolve around the end, all be all: Sunday morning.

The reason why budgets have ballooned in this way is because of the gradual shift in worldview as it pertains to evangelism. The Church has convinced itself that the best way to do ministry is to put on a great show on Sunday morning and attract people in. This is also known as the "seeker-sensitive" model. Make Sunday morning attractive with fog machines, fancy decorations, comfortable seating, music performances, and a short message. And because this is the focus of how churches operate, of course, they are going to put most of their resources into making it as excellent as they can. The problem with that is that it isn't evangelism, it breeds consumerism. Where the average congregant is taught to just come and "get fed," receive and leave, checking that box off in their life and then going about the rest of their week. No wonder church staff across the United States are feeling burned out. This is not how the Church is meant to operate. The Church is not an entertainment source, it is the Body of Christ. Congregants are called to bring themselves, their giftings, their strengths, and callings, and offer them for the edification of the body. But when Church services are crammed up against one another like movie times at your local movie theater, it encourages people to get in, get out and go about their lives, and more times than not leave it at that. Our collective focus has been on what we get from a service, instead of what we bring. Being in the body of Christ means that everyone has an active role in some shape or form, we are not meant to be passive observers. As active members of a church, we are called to tithe, which is indisputably biblical. But when people give, what do they think it is going towards versus what is it going towards?

The Bible is abundantly clear about whom we should be giving to. To give a hint: nowhere does it talk about finances/resources being used for a service or gathering. Instead, it lists out things/people/causes we should be giving to: The poor (Mark 10:21; Proverbs 22:9 & 14:21, Deut. 15:7 and Psalm 112:9), as a form of benevolence (Psalm 41:1; Proverbs 3:27-28; Matthew 5:42 & 25:35-45) and as a blessing to care for those in need (James 2:14-17; Ephesians 4:28; Acts 2:44-

46). All of those listed throughout the Old and New Testament revolve around helping others and specifically assisting those in need. One of the only ways to know if someone needs that is through relationships, which requires work, time, and investment. This is why it is easier to just give your tithe once or twice a month to a church and let them do that work. But what happens if that isn't the work those tithe funds are being used for?

If our focus for tithe money is what kind of show we can put on any given Sunday, the many salaries it requires to put on each weekend, and the building it is being held in, it doesn't leave much of that to the actual work the Bible lines out for us to give towards. When most people give to their church, they assume that those funds are going towards the words they hear from the pulpit on a Sunday about serving the poor, helping the needy, and blessing their community, but what they are giving to are salaries, buildings, decorations, and equipment. There is an element of fairness that needs to be included in this discourse, and that is there are underlying costs that need to be paid to run a church. Bills do need to be paid, utilities need to be covered, food must be bought and budgets for ministries are needed. But once we get past those needs, where do the remaining funds go and what does that say about what we are focused on?

What would it look like to use our resources the way Scripture outlines? Where those that are shouldering the burden of ministry are there because they are serving the church instead of profiting from it? Their presence and work in the church are an act of obedience and a calling rather than occupation and vocation. Making money from a different occupation so that the words they speak from the pulpit aren't marred by the temptation to tickle the largest donor's ears, but instead speaking from a place of conviction unadulterated by money. Serving those that need it the most and dedicating most of the resources the church receives to bless the community and give to them what they need. What if we used the resources given to the Church to bless and serve others, instead of putting on a show? The

Church is meant to be the Body of Christ, where all have a part and a place to be who God created them to be, giving, serving, blessing, and using the resources they are blessed with to assist them in their ministry. Let's get back to that.

Chapter 11

Spiritual Gifts and Empowerment

Brick:

How are spiritual gifts currently being exercised in churches throughout the United States? Why is there a stigma around certain gifts and not others? Where do "common people" within churches exercise their gifts? In what ways are churches stifling the gifts within their congregations? Who is responsible for utilizing the gifts that reside in the body and what are the "qualifications" for using them? What are the consequences for not championing all parts of the body using their gifting/calling/function? Why do most church services only rely on "the few" to serve "the many" and what does that lead to?

Reason for analysis:

Depending on the denomination that someone belongs to, their interaction with spiritual gifts is going to be vastly different. For most that lean more Pentecostal, the use of all spiritual gifts, especially the miraculous, is a common sight. If one leans more

Baptist, their exposure to the use of spiritual gifts is more than likely less than that of a Pentecostal. The focus on spiritual gifts is not to debate what gifts are "active" and which are not, the Bible is clear that all believers are blessed with gifts that are meant to be shared with the body for the means of edification. There will be theological disagreements on both sides which have merit, but there is one thing we can all agree on from what we see in Scripture, and that is we need each other. However, to achieve efficiency and volume, the Church has become an expert at cramming as many services as possible into a weekend and getting people in and out of the church like an effective, well-oiled machine. The reason why this is a problem is that to achieve that kind of efficiency, churches lean on the few to lead and serve the many. Only a handful of people feel empowered to use their spiritual giftings weekend to weekend, while the rest take the comfortable route of allowing leadership to do the spiritual heavy lifting for them. In the current structure of most churches in the United States, congregants come to church to "get something out of it," while the leaders attempt to "give them something to take home." This dynamic could not be further from what the early Church looked like and what it should look like moving forward. Yes, there are leaders and elders within churches, as there should be, but that doesn't mean congregants are destined to only sit on the sideline, consuming content and being served instead of being active participants in the body. Though it may be what congregants think they want, believers are only the full version of God's intention for their life when they are fully exercising the identity given to them by Christ and that includes but is not limited to the use of the gifts given to them for the edification of the body they belong to.

Discussing the complexity and expression of spiritual gifts can be difficult at times. First, as Christians, we are trained to not talk about ourselves positively because it can be interpreted as pride or ego. And secondly, not all Christians agree on what gifts are active, what those expressions should look like, or how they all fit together in the body. The emphasis of this chapter is not to debate the latter, it is to discuss the function of spiritual gifts in the body and where the church in the United States is sorely lacking in the execution of them. When the Lord blesses us with something, it is always meant for us to use that thing for His glory, whatever that may look like. Following that truth, spiritual gifts are not only a part of that, but they may also be the core of what that truth means.

Out of the gate, we as Christians should acknowledge that all people who claim Christ and who are born again, are blessed with spiritual gifts. Some are more "front-facing" than others, but that doesn't mean the gifts that aren't are worth any less or have any less impact in the Kingdom. When the Lord gives us these gifts, we are called to use them. Whether the gifts are built into our personalities or are new traits developed through spiritual maturity, the exercise of them must be intentional. Whatever someone's gifting is, the enemy is just as aware of what that gifting is as we are, maybe sometimes even more. There will be opposition in those areas that take many forms, but our ability to seek strength, wisdom, discernment, and will through the Holy Spirit enable us to use our giftings to the fullest. If everyone that follows Christ and is born again has spiritual gifts, that means every single believer has a role to play while they are here on this earth. If that person is drawing breath, they have purpose and meaning in their life, simply by acknowledging that they have been blessed with a gift that is meant to be shared.

In Ephesians 4:11-13, Paul says, "So Christ himself gave the apostles, the prophets, the evangelists, the pastors, and teachers, to equip his people for works of service, so that the body of Christ may be built up until we all reach unity in the faith and in the knowledge of the Son of God and become mature, attaining to the whole measure of the fullness of Christ." Within these passages, there is plenty to break down, but the main line drawn from these words to the church of Ephesus is that the purpose of spiritual gifts is for the body of Christ to be built up. Another word for building up that we see in Scripture is to "edify." In this specific case, Paul is telling them that the role of the apostles, the prophets, the evangelists, the pastors, and teachers is to equip the Church so that they can build each other up and achieve true unity. This is no small task and is of utmost importance to the health of the body of Christ.

He continues in verses 14-16 saying, "Then we will no longer be infants, tossed back and forth by the waves, and blown here and there by every wind of teaching and by the cunning and craftiness of people in their deceitful scheming. Instead, speaking the truth in love, we will grow to become in every respect the mature body of him who is the head, that is, Christ. From him, the whole body, joined and held together by every supporting ligament, grows, and builds itself up in love, as each part does its work." How Paul is describing the unification of the body further points to the truth that each person has a role to play. Each individual has a gift, a talent, or something to offer the body that is unique to them. But people have been convinced that going to church is all about what they "get out of it" while the authors of the New Testament say the exact opposite when talking about how the Church is meant to operate together.

It isn't good enough to feel content knowing that the Lord has given you a gift or talent, we are called directly to use them. In 1 Peter 4:10, it says, "Each of you should use whatever gift you have received to serve others, as faithful stewards of God's grace in its various forms." And in 1 Timothy 4:14, it says, "Do not neglect your gift, which was given you through prophecy when the body of elders laid their hands on you." In that specific verse, Paul is talking directly to Timothy about the specific calling he had to pastor the local church that was entrusted to him, but that direct truth can be spoken directly into our lives as well. If we choose not to use our gift, it is exactly that: a choice. This means if we choose not to use what was given to us, we are neglecting the use of that gift. The parable of the talents where the one servant who chose to bury his talent instead of investing it was sent out to the weeping and gnashing of teeth because of his disobedience illustrates the same point. The Lord takes our negligence and apathy towards our gifting seriously, and we should too. One reading this may be convinced they should use their spiritual gift but may not know what it is or what spiritual gifts are.

There are a few distinctions between spiritual gifts that help believers understand what role they play in the body of Christ. The first is distinguishing between "common" and "miraculous" spiritual gifts. These names are not marking the importance of the two, common does not mean less impactful or boring, it is meant to help define the natural and supernatural differences between them. To read and see the list of spiritual gifts, 1 Corinthians 12:1-11, Romans 12, 1 Peter 4:7-11, and Ephesians 4 are good places to start. There they are listed and defined within the context of the passages they are written. The common gifts are described as, "wisdom, knowledge, faith, serving, teaching, encouragement, giving, leadership, mercy, administration, hospitality and service" and the supernatural gifts are listed as "healing, prophecy, speaking in tongues, interpreting tongues and discernment." How these are expressed and what it looks like will be unique to the person that has them. Two people can have the same gift, but have it look completely different in its execution.

Every person that claims Christ as their Lord and Savior and follows Him has a spiritual gift. They may not know it or what it looks like, but that doesn't mean it isn't there, it just means it hasn't been discovered yet. Understanding how you are designed and what that looks like in your life is part of a journey that the Lord puts all believers on, and these things can change with age, maturity, and wisdom. One beneficial part of being a Christian is that the use of spiritual gifts is not exclusive to church leaders or influencers, but to the entire body. And even if you don't have one of the other spiritual gifts, that doesn't mean you can't call on the Holy Spirit to use them in situations that call for it.

This dynamic is known as the difference between "Macro" and "Atmospheric" gifts. Macro gifts are the traits that we are born with. When we wake up in the morning that is who we are, and no circumstance or life situation would change that. An example of this is someone who has the gift of administration. Someone with the gift of administration is organized in all aspects of their life and it comes naturally to them. They can organize people and details with ease and whether it is in the context of a board room or putting together a snack schedule for the pee-wee soccer team, everything they do is blessed by their gift of administration. This phenomenon is true for all of us. We all have traits that make us who we are and could fall under one of the "common" spiritual gift categories. But what is exciting about being a Christian and having the Holy Spirit, is that there may be life situations that arise where other spiritual gifts are needed but you don't necessarily have that gift come naturally to you. This is where "Atmospheric" gifting comes in. Within the power of the Holy Spirit, we have the power and authority to ask the Holy Spirit to bless us with a gift to address specific problems and events that we encounter where that is needed. You don't have to have all the gifts within your personality to use them when needed.

Once someone has figured out how they are wired, what gets them excited, and starts looking for opportunities to use their gifts, some internal conflict can present itself to prevent them from moving forward. Having the confidence or boldness to step out and begin using a gift or newly discovered talent is rare. Oftentimes, people will look for a leader to champion them and encourage them to step out in faith to start using it. Even though a gift may be a part of who you are, the application of that gift will require work, patience, and refinement the more you use it, so stay patient with yourself through that process. If someone doesn't have natural confidence in their abilities or have someone in their corner positively pushing them to try it out, it can be difficult to evade the self-doubt and insecurity that undoubtedly will arise.

When believers are trying out new giftings and meet any kind of resistance, the natural inclination is to give up. This can lead to apathy or laziness in being okay with the "intercessor" paradigm. In the Old Testament, the Levite Priests oversaw communing with God on behalf of the entire Israelite people. They would go through a cleansing process and engage with the Holy of Holies to worship Him, to ask for guidance on how or where to lead Israel, to ask forgiveness both individually and collectively, and all kinds of other things that common Israelites were prohibited to do for themselves. Every day Israelites had to depend on the priests to be an intercessor for them and speak to God on their behalf. When Jesus died on the cross, he became a permanent intercessor between us and the Father. Because we are covered by His blood and His sacrifice, we can have a relationship with the Father without another human being involved. All believers have direct access to the Father, and we no longer need a priest to go to Him on our behalf. Followers of Christ who are insecure about their relationship with God or using their gifts can fall into laziness where they let their leaders engage with God for them on a Sunday morning, but don't engage with the Lord themselves. This paradigm will prevent believers from using their spiritual gifts because they feel like they don't "have" to. Some congregants have found a way to overcome insecurity and fear and begin using their gifts but still have internal struggles that can prevent them from using them consistently.

One of the ways that people discourage themselves from stepping out of their comfort zones is because of past trauma or hurt, especially in the context of the church. When people volunteer their time, energy, and resources to the church it is easy for a leader to 'use them'. The reason why this terminology is negative everywhere but the church is because it has a connotation of using someone until there is nothing left. If boundaries and self-care aren't established by the leaders of a ministry that has a volunteer force, it is easy for people to begin serving with a zeal and passion that ends up being snuffed out by overuse, under-appreciation, and a feeling of being used. If someone has experienced ministry in that way before, they are far more reluctant to engage in a role within the church again, hence the neglect of their gift. Overcoming this type of hurt and burnout is not easy, nor is it common. To climb out of the depths of the emotions that come from situations like this is heavy work and often requires counseling, introspection, and healing that takes time. Implementing your gifting to the fullest extent of God's intention for your life requires purity of heart that can only come from the clarity of the Holy Spirit's guidance. Oftentimes people have the willingness and the heart to explore the depths of their gifting, but the commitment of time can be a hurdle that some refuse to jump over.

As with anything we commit to, there will be a demand for time and effort to fully engage in the areas that we are called to. In life, especially in a consumerist culture, there are always places to be, things to do, and people to see. This means that to use our gifting, one must choose to sacrifice time that could be spent doing other things to serve and edify the body with the calling bestowed upon them. People are reluctant to commit to anything in this era, from a place of not wanting to miss out on anything and not wanting to be locked down to something if our fancy and attention are drawn elsewhere. The commitment to pouring into the body of Christ is going to be tested by many distractions and things or people that want our attention which requires us to fight our own internal battles to keep our focus on what we are called to do, regardless of the noise around us that constantly pulls us into different directions. But these internal struggles that constantly gnaw at our innermost being are multiplied by outside forces that seek to distract us from the walk we are called to.

Many variables come into play when answering the question of why people aren't using their giftings within their local body. As discussed above, that can be internal insecurity that arises in the individual when comparing themselves with other believers, specifically the most public and elevated leaders. But this can also happen due to external circumstances as well.

People can be discouraged at times because they compare their gifts with others in the body, or even worse with leaders of their church. They can identify that they have a similar gift as a leader in the church, but obviously are not as refined or well-practiced as they are in using them. Just like anything in our lives, we must use our gifts and develop within them to use them at their full capacity. But when comparing ourselves with other believers, we can be discouraged from using them at all. How leaders cultivate an environment for all congregants to use their spiritual gifts is delicate and requires intentional attention.

An element that can sometimes be overlooked when talking about the leap of faith and confidence it requires to step out into your gifting is that of spiritual warfare. It can be easy to over-spiritualize some elements of this phenomenon, but there is validity to the enemy wanting to discourage people from ever using their gifts. One aspect of the external struggle we fight against is the enemy trying to circumvent us from ever using our gift often enough to really impact the kingdom in any meaningful way. These attacks can come to fruition in any number of ways. They can come in the form of discouragement, critical words from others, feelings of not feeling good enough, or any other internal insecurity and virtually any other tactic that will attempt to convince you that you are not worthy of using the gift that you have been given. The way that we think about ourselves, the Church, and our place in it is under a constant barrage of doubt, struggle, and discouragement. The battlefield of the mind is not something to be taken lightly, and the enemy knows that if they can succeed in discouraging us, the odds of us not even trying to use our gift are high.

Human and sinful nature can easily take over our thought life if we aren't taking thoughts captive and being mindful of where we let them wander. Obviously, leaders are meant to use their gifts as a part of their leadership of the church, but enabling others to come alongside them and use their gifting as well requires humility and self-confidence which is difficult to find in most churches today. Part of our sinful nature is to fall into insecurity and pride when presented with others who are gifted or maybe even more gifted than us within our congregations. The mind can easily wander to "what if people see their gift and like them more than they like me"? Or "what if the church wants to replace me with that person and I lose my job"? These questions and ones like it can lead to the suppression of other people in the body using their God-given gifts and talents because leaders are paranoid about being replaced or devalued. All these mental lapses happen to all of us because it is built into our sinful nature. To not act in this way requires wisdom, maturity, and mental discipline that can only come from the Holy Spirit.

Sometimes, leaders can identify talent in others, and they do want them to explore and use them for the glory of God and the betterment of the congregation. But the external struggle they find themselves in is the inability for them to find a place for them to plug in. Utilizing resources and being creative in the expression of the gifts of others can be a daunting task. It generally comes with new outlets and changes that require time, effort, and resources that the church may not immediately have. It has been said that within the ministry, you should constantly either be reinventing yourself or your ministry and that is because people are always changing. Most of the time, finding new avenues to plug people in that weren't previously there requires patience and persistence that pushes through the boundaries of constraint that comes from "doing things the way we always have." The willingness it requires to evolve and grow, based on the giftings and talents that reside within your congregation is an artform that the most careful of leaders must balance on a usual basis. To get people involved and use their gifts, space must be made for them to do so.

Developing new ministries for people to use their strengths, gifts and talents must be intentional. It is easy for humans to fall into the status quo and continue to do things the way we always have because that is where results are "known." The problem with running a ministry that way is that it tends to have a diminishing return over time. Things that once worked with great effect begin to wane in their effectiveness. People stop getting as excited as they once were, the passion that was once used is no longer there and is replaced by a monotony of doing things because we "have to." Building out these new ministries and ways of utilizing gifts and talents, requires humility and tenacity to see them to fruition. People must feel championed by those in leadership to fully invest themselves in their respective ministries.

When people already struggle with internal struggles about the use of their gift, if there is an external pressure to not use it as well, it is virtually guaranteed that they will remain in the pews, silently watching others pour into them, but not being an active participant in the kingdom like they were designed to be. People choose the path of least resistance, and this is no exception. But the body is designed for all people to feel empowered and use the gifts and talents that the Lord has given them for His glory. All believers, regardless of the type of gifting, have been knighted by Jesus to be active participants in the body, by being the person He has called them to be. But one question persists, especially for churches that have hundreds, if not thousands of congregants. How do we incorporate everyone's gifts?

There isn't just one blanket answer that answers that question for everyone. How this question is answered is going to vary from person to person, congregation to congregation, and leader to leader. Similarities may exist and ideas can (and should) be shared between churches for how this looks, but there isn't a box that everyone must fit in. Some principles can be implemented that will lead to this type of culture.

The first way that we glean from Scripture that this can be accomplished is through discipleship. When well-seasoned leaders choose to pour into the next generation, expounding on the lessons they learned while in ministry can help guide people into using their giftings as well. This type of discipleship should lead to the empowerment of the person being discipled to go out and use the gifts/talents that reside within them. Within this dynamic, the person doing the discipling should be actively looking for ways that their disciple can take "low risk" opportunities and try out the things they learn from the development they gain by reading the Word and other Scriptural references, praying and words of wisdom given to them from others. But these low-risk endeavors must be led by the Holy Spirit and intentionally pursued without the expectation of worldly success. Oftentimes we as broken humans will use worldly metrics to judge whether a ministry is successful and that is an extremely misguided way to approach that type of judgment.

If we use worldly metrics to analyze and judge the success of ministries, oftentimes our ministries will end up looking like the world. We must approach our creativity to do things differently, while also having an open-handed mentality that says, "if this doesn't work or this stops working, I'm willing to adjust or move on as needed." If we hold onto a ministry beyond its expiration date, it often only leads to frustration and angst that can only be resolved by obeying and shutting it down. The way that we develop and build ministries must be led by the Holy Spirit and run by those that are gifted and called to run them. When we attempt to force a square peg into a round hole, the health of the overall ministry can grow stagnant. Implementing everyone's spiritual gifts within the body must be done with great care, intentionality, and creativity.

A lot has been said about spiritual gifts in theological circles and those debates will continue until Christ returns. Where people fall when it comes to whether supernatural gifts are active or not is irrelevant to this conversation. What matters is that all believers realize that they are specifically gifted and designed by God to fit into the body by using their strengths, gifts, and talents for the Kingdom. Once that truth has been realized, leaders are charged with the task of equipping those they are entrusted to lead with the tools, knowledge, and opportunity to use those giftings in a way that will lead to the edification of the body. As leaders empower their people into new frontiers and push them to be who Christ intended them to become, they must creatively and intentionally provide spaces and grace for them to work out what that looks like and encourage them along the way. And lastly, and most importantly, stay faithful to the leading of the Holy Spirit, asking the Lord to open and close doors as He sees fit, enabling those around us to flourish into the powerful body of Christ that they are meant to become.

Afterword

Certainty is a dangerous place to inhabit. There are many times and places throughout Scripture where God deals in absolutes. The Ten Commandments, listing of the Fruit of the Spirit, calling those who follow Christ to love God and to love others. But there are far more times when things aren't completely clear. Treating the Bible like it is an instruction manual to follow one extreme or another is dangerous and oftentimes leads to people getting hurt.

In college, I had a professor named Brad Harper that explained these complex topics of discussion as "Living in the Tension" and that has stuck with me to this day. Most things in life are not absolute. They are multi-layered, multi-faceted, and require a certain level of nuanced thinking and humility that can be difficult to master. It's okay to not be "sure." As stated in the introduction, if we agree on the core of orthodoxy as believers, all secondary doctrine is up for debate.

God is not afraid of you asking questions. He isn't afraid of your doubt or your unbelief. His love for you doesn't waver because your experiences, hurt, trauma or abuse drove you away from wanting to engage with Him or the Church for a time. While we are still living, we are going to encounter many different situations we couldn't foresee that will challenge what we believe, why we believe it and how that is going to impact our lives moving forward. The Lord welcomes this process and is not intimidated by it. This quote from Bertrand sums this thought up well, "We put our faith in the person of Christ, not in the teaching of the church. Does this mean that doctrine has no value? Of course not. But we are not saved by being right; we are saved by being His."

We must come to a place of humility, where we can accept the premise that we could be wrong. That even if we come to a place of sureness about a topic, we are still willing to listen to other points of view, evaluate the merit without defensiveness and be open to changing our minds. The world is constantly pulling us into extremes and telling us that the only way to live is to embody one of them. There are core tenets of belief that we should keep set in stone but with the rest hold with a loose grip in an open palm. If God wanted to, He could have just given us a binary set of standards to live by, a strict code of dos and don'ts and see how we do. But He didn't. The ones He does give us, we should heed with the utmost seriousness, but with the rest, there will never be a way to be one hundred percent sure you are right until you meet Him face to face and you can ask Him.

The best place to see this in Scripture is seeing how Jesus lived and taught those who followed Him. What a better time than when you are the incarnate son of God, walking among your beloved to clear up any confusion, give them specific instructions and lay out a detailed plan for their lives. In reality, we see Jesus do the exact opposite. We see him tell parables and ask questions of those close with him and the random passerby alike. People ask him questions and He answers them with another question. A reader of the gospels can easily get frustrated with Jesus' lack of directedness in those situations. But that doesn't mean that Jesus never was direct or clear. Most of the time that Jesus was being clear, it was when He was rebuking those who were sure of themselves and their understanding of the order of things.

Jesus asks upwards of three hundred questions in the four gospels that try to encapsulate three whole years of ministry. Those around Him ask him upwards of one hundred. Asking and evaluating good questions is an important part of our process. The entire New Testament breaks down the logic of what "once was" and ushers in the Kingdom of Heaven upon Christ's arrival and continues with the Holy Spirit to this day. Evaluating the workings of this world has been happening since the dawn of time and will continue to be as long as humans are alive on this planet. This has largely been done through the process of deep thought, contemplation and discussion about the complexity that comes from the life that we live. To live in a constant state of certainty is foolishness.

God brings about divine inspiration through a multitude of sources. The list of all of those sources would be too extensive to write here, but He speaks to all of us through different methods. You don't need a high priest to intercede between you and God any longer, Jesus is our ultimate high priest that justifies us before the Father. This means that we all have access to the same Holy Spirit, the same power, inspiration, and wisdom if we seek it from Him. These questions that you have asked, are asking and will continue to ask are a part of the process. Not knowing everything continually brings us to His feet. Discovery is one of the keys to intimacy.

As we continue to seek understanding, we will continue to seek Him. And as we seek Him, our intimacy and relationship with Him will only grow deeper. If the approach we take when addressing these hard issues is to edify and build His bride, there will only be continuously expanding capacity for more. The end of one hard question doesn't bring fulfillment, if anything, it generally leads to more hard questions. This is the beauty in pursuing both a fully known and unknowable creator. We live in constant tension.

Finishing this book is just a starting point. It just starts to scratch the surface of tough questions that the Church encounters on a daily basis. These topics are worthy of deep thought, contemplation, discourse, and resolution. Don't get stuck in the ethereal world. How you implement and apply your conclusions will have positive ripple effects throughout your church and your community. But there will be more questions to answer, new issues that are pressing, and current events that demand your response. And my hope is that by reading this book, it has shown you a way to evaluate your view of the Church in a healthy way brick by brick.

About Kharis Publishing:

Kharis Publishing, an imprint of Kharis Media LLC, is a leading Christian and inspirational book publisher based in Aurora, Chicago metropolitan area, Illinois. Kharis' dual mission is to give voice to under-represented writers (including women and first-time authors) and equip orphans in developing countries with literacy tools. That is why, for each book sold, the publisher channels some of the proceeds into providing books and computers for orphanages in developing countries so that these kids may learn to read, dream, and grow. For a limited time, Kharis Publishing is accepting unsolicited queries for nonfiction (Christian, self-help, memoirs, business, health and wellness) from qualified leaders, professionals, pastors, and ministers. Learn more at: About Us - Kharis Publishing - Accepting Manuscript

CPSIA information can be obtained
at www.ICGtesting.com
Printed in the USA
BVHW030539060822
643805BV00002B/3